The Mercy Seat

The Mercy Seat

*Collected & New Poems
1967–2001*

NORMAN DUBIE

 Copper
Canyon
Press

Printed in the United States of America.

Copper Canyon Press wishes to thank Leo Kenney for the use of *Rapport III*. Our thanks also to Janet Huston and William Merchant Pease for making it possible to use Mr. Kenney's work.

Grateful acknowledgment is made to the following publications in which some of these poems have appeared:

AGNI, American Poetry Review, Antaeus, Antioch Review, Argos (*Wales*)*, The Black Warrior Review, Blue Moon News, The Cincinnati Review, Colorado Review, Crazyhorse, English Language in Transition, Fence, Field, The Georgia Review, Gettysburg Review, The Gramercy Review, Grilled Flowers, Hayden's Ferry Review, The Iowa Review, Ironwood, The Kenyon Review, Manoa, Marilyn, Maverick Magazine, Mississippi Review, New England Review, New Virginia Review, The New Yorker, The North American Review, The Ohio Review, The Pacific Review, The Paris Review, Ploughshares, Poetry, Porch, Quarterly West, Santa Monica Review, Seneca Review, The Southern Review, Telescope, Western Humanities Review, Yellow Brick Road,* and The Recursos Press (Santa Fe, New Mexico).

Special acknowledgment is made to Porch Publications, who first published *Odalisque in White*.

Special acknowledgment is also made to The Ingram Merrill Foundation, The John Simon Guggenheim Memorial Foundation, and the National Endowment for the Arts for their generous support.

Special acknowledgment is made to the Cosmorati Press, who first published *The Amulet*.

Copper Canyon Press is in residence under the auspices of the Centrum Foundation at Fort Worden State Park in Port Townsend, Washington. Centrum sponsors artist residencies, education workshops for Washington State students and teachers, blues, jazz, and fiddle tunes festivals, classical music performances, and The Port Townsend Writers' Conference.

LIBRARY OF CONGRESS CATALOGING-IN-PUBLICATION DATA

Dubie, Norman, 1945–
The mercy seat: collected and new poems, 1967–2001 / Norman Dubie.
  p. cm.
ISBN 1-55659-212-4 (alk. paper)
1. Title.
PS3554.U255 M47 2001
811'.54 — DC21   2001001018

SECOND EDITION

COPPER CANYON PRESS
Post Office Box 271
Port Townsend, Washington 98368
www.coppercanyonpress.org

for H.H., the 14th Dalai Lama;
for Hannah & Kaya

Contents

PART TWO

Poems 1991–2001

The Mercy Seat

The Friary at Blossom,
Prologue & Instructions

The pond lilies are like little executions
over the water, the flat physical collars
of aristocrats, and the cords that lunge
for the bottom. The yellow perch circling
the impeccable underneath of farewell, government,
and mud in April.

The image of a horse diving into water
ignores the wild dogs up on the cliff,
their failure to join the horse and everything
in pursuit off the edge, passed by birds
and other flying things. This is like your decision
to continue with me out into the firm and steaming
pussywillows. We laugh.

Thomas Wyatt in the Tower was brought a pigeon
daily by a gray cat;
this supply saved him from starvation. But you
must imagine how it was for him, a poet,
in a stone room with blood and feathers on his
shirt and the gray cat on the prowl who pounced
in grass and who dragged it back
to this man who once dismantled flowers in his lap
and sang to women songs that were happy and sad.
I think he became that cat each morning
that springtime
out crawling for his breakfast in the grass; I think
the cat remained the cat, a poor prisoner to reaction

but very fast.

—1967

PART ONE
Poems 1967–1990

Wandering, estranged and lonely, he saw a wild pig
covered with mud, and a wagon full of demons. First
he stretched his bow but then put it aside. It is not an
obstacle, but a matter of betrothal to the times...

I CHING

We are on each other's hands
who care

JOHN BERRYMAN

Popham of the New Song

for Pamela Stewart

Neither all nor any angels arrive in the mind where
The spruce and fir shake at the sun in the morning
Spilling some yellow over the water. Some yellow
And the motion of next to no motion
Across the rocks, a salt-air, the old oceans
Return us, slowly tug us, along the familiar fiction

Of childhood. We were children. No longer.
This is the beginning of something
Not given, hopefully, too often: the present
Moment. No little engine in a little boat. But the
Bucket with a hole in it. From the well to the house.
The loss of water like a problem; the referendum that

Doesn't make an ocean. It has lost all confidence
In us. *A last essay in a bowl.*
We are sorry but the salvages were wages.
It's the way the little clams
In their black beds peep and then stare
At the crocuses, now, up and alarmed, everywhere.

There were two books not yet dusted with a feather.
Not yet books as books in rooms.
The liars are all out on the smallest branch
That cracks the window. Around the cellar windows
There is a black sticky paper. The green of the pine
This time is saying to the winter: Give it up, give it up.

A man sits back and relinquishes his childhood, his child's
Childhood, his child. No longer carrying clear water
In a small cup. One foot before the other. He wonders

If the bright color of a bird breaking from the thicket
Will be enough. This is not the beginning or the end
Of just one or the other season. This is a man

Who believes that a child has grown and grown but
Never in the mind. In the mind under the boughs
She has just weakened.
And, now, bring the towels and basins. The fresh linen
And ribbons.
It's evening. And neither all nor any of the angels arrive here

In the rooms where a child is being clothed in jewels and dresses.
The wooden boats knocking around
Outside like two old women calling for a cat who's died
                    Out in the first mud and forsythia. Far outside.

        II.

And so a man I love says fifteen years is all he has;
And so I say to the man I love: A great wheel
Made of wood and iron
Will make but one revolution in fifteen years, crossing
Fields outside Odessa, ropes and songs and mules
Making it an infinite nostalgia of a white animal.

Do men in bright blouses surround a senseless element.
The way a horn is tipped
Spilling squash, winter melons, and huge black
Leaves that are smoked in lodges near a stream.
The coronary like naked children standing in a pond.
Of forms, I tell him, the body is profound.

It is of bread and water that people die.
The will-to-change
Lugs a piano on its back.
And retires, humid
At midnight with a glass of milk. It hits the sack.

This mover of objects down the stairs says there is
Only one piano in its life and it is black.

We dressed the child and said, perhaps, that two friends
Died. There is no wife.
The measure of her waist is equal to the radius
Of the wheel above or the wrist of the ambiguous child.
Who was put in a boat. Who waved good-bye.
The will-to-change is a likable vertebrate. Surprised?

Is that what we mean when we say they die.
Or is it that we're all alike. The watercolors
Of then and now. Your father in Russia. The clover, or
The shock-tactics of lucid flowers all wired
Into bundles and found
On the chests of dead Sicilian children. A clover only

Of the mind. I mind! Who tripped
Us on the stairs.
A picture of little hope in a prospect of flowers.
A marvelous fall on the stairs and all the little hammers
And teeth of the will-to-change broken, scattered
Across the floor. I will not go!

To Peoria this time friend. Or Odessa or Romania.
Nothing will? Romania? Margaret and Rita
Are children on the stairs, and all afternoon they comb
              Each other's hair. They don't believe in me or you.

III. OPPOSITION

Four farmers seen through an open window falling asleep
While playing cards
In the very early morning at a small railway station
In Belgium. And so poetry wins a few hearts.
This is a small boy's way of insisting on adventure,
But with the violence of a great-grandmother who spits.

We are defeated by the commonplace splendor of a battle
Between night and late evening.
The figure for the struggle could be a virgin
On a porch shaking out a tablecloth while calling
To the birds. Come and eat! Come and eat!
Vigorously shaking her tablecloth; all the birds

Fleeing to the nearest tree. Can nothing be done
Right in my story.
The rare black Auk is resting on her eggs.
There is a beautiful tall blonde in a flapping dress
Stepping from a train in Belgium. There is an open
Window through which she sees four farmers playing

Cards while looking out an open window at her knees.
Somewhere between them there's a sheet
Of hotel stationery carried by a breeze. Somewhere between what?
She and the farmers? Or her knees? In the congress of degrees of
            slow speech
There is the great black Auk about to say something.

"All across Europe I hear women dying in childbirth."
Or, "Up in the tree the owl and the nightingale
Speak to each other and tremble but don't sleep."
Poetry can win a few hearts. A woman stands in a tub:
You think one breast is smaller than the other.
But then you're not sure. You've fallen

In love. There is one idea
That is easily
Released with just a finger and a thumb.
Behind the virgin the screen door slams just once
And all the birds are coming down out of the trees
And not very secretly. The great black Auk

Is screaming for joy. Her lovely young! Things are getting
Better for my story. We're back where it had begun. One of

The farmers leans and says to the youngest, "Did you see
That letter fly between her knees." They are drunk.

IV. LES PAPILLONS NOIRS

A black sedan draws along the woods stopping
For occasional white daffodils; there are still
Some patches of snow. The two women looking
To both sides of the road. One says, "Emma Bovary
Had a beehive below her window and the bees
Circling in the sunlight would sometimes strike

Against the window as fast yellow balls."
The other says, "Once after some winter rains everything
Froze and to take water from the well I would
First with slack rope and a flatiron in the bucket
Drop the bucket to open the water. Seldom have
I felt physical."

"And then the shadows of evening are falling." Dreamlike.
"The triumphs are, of course, never physical."
The two women still cruising along the woods.
The younger remembers the Viscount's arm red
And twitching in mud and straw by the wagon. The first
Clear desire to touch a muscle. Once

In the war her mother wrestled a large leg away
From a starving horse. It was
Winter and she saw for the first time those black butterflies,
Those light ashes floating at the edge of everything
When your eyes are sore and tired. She also
Remembered her brother who drilled with the militia

On Sundays. Boys just up in the trees
Cheering and insulting; all of their legs dangling but
Not belonging to the scene or to the promise of
Anything simple like white daffodils in new dirt at evening.

(Catching minnows with a colander.) This is the younger's
Story and going only from one thought to another.

What provokes the birds in the morning is her man.
At the sink he vomits, the small waist moving regularly,
Poisoned with mayonnaise he had made with his father
On Saturday. The men make the mayonnaise on Saturday.
All the eggs and peppers. The bowls of ice and green cigars
From Vaubyessard. The smoke

Like April now steaming in the woods at evening. Black
Butterflies. White daffodils. A red muscle. Like monks
Sitting down to copy. Two women bent over flowers
On a newspaper. They say, "What to keep.
What to throw away."

     v.

for R.P. Blackmur

There are the countless, returning New England widows and
Spinsters. They are returning from the shed with wood
Or kerosene. They follow in their own footsteps
A course, soft but exact, like reapers with knives
Bare to the waist crossing a yellow field.
They know their lives, early and late, and talk peacefully

To the elderly hen who lives in straw, why not in the attic.
"I buried our garden last week." A blue face
With a buttercup under each eye.
The painted face of a woman laid out
In a stone house; trying to raise herself
Just with her elbows: her elbows looking more

Like the back legs of a cricket or a fly.
Emily Dickinson's job was to lay out knives
In the seminary dining hall in the morning
And to wash and dry them at night, counting them twice,

While returning them to the purple drawers. Running to her
Room under the curfew bells. She said

Her father never snored. He thought
She would hide some of her letters
In the big bushes by the vegetables and marigolds.
There was an interview with a pigeon.
Twice I dreamed I was a Jew in China
Eating blue leaves off branches with roots.

So these women were young and knew young men
From Amherst and Salem. Young men watched
From windows walking in circles under elms and oaks.
The wheeling princes of rank and order
Come to visit first with the father and then
The daughters. "The mysterious beauty of someone red

And, yes, the energy even of his stutter."
Well, I said they are all, now, stepping high
And precisely through snow and back from
The shed. Maybe, there's even a ghost or two.
In summer represented by lightning striking
The iron rooster on the roof of the barn.

They know their lives, early and late, and set out
Knives in seminaries and, nevertheless,
Die a natural death. And, nevertheless, value coal
          With alabaster. And suffer affliction like an insect.

VI. THE JOYOUS, THE LAKE

How two women can be the same, for instance, in Poland
On a wharf at a lake where naked women are
Being instructed by soldiers to walk quickly along
To the end of the wharf, at last, every two of them
Are passed a blanket to share as they step down
Into the steady boats. It's a wet October day.

Some cry. Some sing. *Naked you are beside*
Yourself. These pairs of women on the hard benches
In the boats are like that, and especially at the width
Of each boat: two large middle-aged women working
The oars, their blankets fallen to the floor
Of the boat. Pulling it across, not sisters,

Occasionally looking over a shoulder. In the middle
Of the lake it rains on everyone briefly; all the songs
Now are to help the women rowing.
The sleeves of the soldiers are of red wool and they are
Also miserable. They are
Like a corpse in soil included in the scene.

Pastor Cruikshank looks out over the lake. I offer
Him dry matches. I say that order is for the birds
If it appears as the survival of restraints
After the feelings it meant to contain are no longer felt
By anyone on the face of the earth. He says, Well, and for
That matter all the birds are in Marseille. The Nazis in Warsaw.

And we, my boy, are on the shore of a cold lake. Perhaps, all
Feelings are the birth of the shape they take. Now, I thought
Of that, but made it his speech. Please, reach me down
That book, that jar, or the feeling that runs
The nude in the morning away from the water up the sloping
Lawn to the cottage with a yellow gate. An air or melody.

The Pastor says that Puritans gathered on a beach
In their capes and looked back across the ocean
Remembering the crazy bobbin on a nail of bone,
The green milk in the shade,
And the green manure in the barns outside a village.
What color was the pond? That too was a mistake.

And then he left drawing a thumb across his leg. That means
Nothing to us, early or late. The women in the boat

Were the last delay of a dream aria with water. *A bird*
Drops down from a tree in the sun in Marseille.

VII. SONG

A bird drops down from a tree in the sun in Marseille.
This is a bitter poem. This is a poem that meant
To be an admission of love to a woman
Whom it admits it loves. *This is a bitter poem.*
This is a poem of love for a woman and a bird both

Dropping out of a tree in the sun; yes, in Marseille.
And actually I'm now just writing this poem. You
On the other hand are just now reading this poem.
From here on it is already written for you; not yet written
For me. Why do I continue with it?

Because you are inseparable from the woman this poem
Has a love for, and the bird, also; almost down from the tree.
This poem loves a rotting boat in a green cove, some
Daffodils, and a young Nazi lacing a boot by a dead truck
By the lake in a cold rain. He is looking at a copy

Of Heine. If this bothers you. (The poem's affection
For the soldier.) Then the rest of the poem is not written
For you. It is a poem that couldn't love
The woman I love. It is a poem I couldn't love but
It is a poem of love, I think, despite either of us.

The young Nazi finishes lacing
His boot by making a careful bow. Now is that
Altogether surprising. It is a surprise to the woman
This is written for who is sometimes, also, the only
Person reading this poem. Yes, she could be you.

This is the achievement of this poem. That it is
Now finally speaking just to *you*. This is
No longer a bitter poem; no longer a poem
                    that could continue!

In the Dead of the Night

for Weingarten

There's the story of me sitting in the grass in the dark
With the dark cat, for hours she has been at it,
Stalking fireflies and sometimes falling
On her back, sometimes her jaws working
Very fast. For a moment I thought of
A few friends; only for a moment,
I thought. And then up the stairs to bed,
Thinking then of the old rabbi in Poland, large
And in a forest poking with a stick
In his own black manure for the gold tooth
He swallowed at a feast.
I remembered a photograph of the lights of Dresden
During a blizzard, one old bus making it
Slowly along a warehouse. For a moment
I thought it was a dream, only for a moment I did
Dream: the cat entering by a large window leaps
Onto the bed.
She strains and vomits hundreds of dead bugs,
Some green and black,
Then solid areas of light, yellow, next
To the sad half-lights that miss and strike again.
Not a constellation going out in your lap.
What can't you make out: the Great Bear
Hobbled with a short ladder, or a plow blade,
Or perhaps just a whole city impoverished but for
Shovels. The story of its light
As the last insect tries the last light.
And a rabbi dancing in the forest, he spins
Twice around and then unwinds, his arms flying
Laughing and crying; look sharply at the hand that
Is most above him, lovely man, something very
Black, something very bright, from inside him.

For Randall Jarrell, 1914–1965

What the wish wants to see, it sees.

All the dead are eating little yellow peas
Off knives under the wing of an owl
While the living run around, not aimlessly, but
Like two women in white dresses gathering
Hymnbooks out on a lawn with the first
Drops of rain already falling on them.

Once, I wrote a sudden and enormous sentence
At the bottom of a page in a notebook
Next to a sketch of a frog. The sentence
Described the gills of a sunfish
As being the color of cut rhubarb, or
Of basil if it is dried in a bundle
In a red kitchen with the last winter light
Showing it off, almost purple.

Anything approaching us we try to understand, say,
Like a lamp being carried up a lane at midnight.

Jeremy Taylor knew it watching an orange leaf
Go down a stream.
Self-taught, it came to us, I believe,
As old age to a panther who's about to
Spring from one branch to another, but suddenly
Thinks better of it.
She says to us from her tree,
"Please, one world at a time!" and leaps —

Making it, which could mean,
Into this world or some other. And between.

Indian Summer

for Richard Howard

1.

No one will come with water and white rags. No one
Will bother with stones or ferns.
These are dead settlers
After the massacre in the early morning. The sun

Has just begun to bake hard red caps on the heads
Of the children. Around their throats there will
Be necklaces. There are sleeves and bibs and over
The mother's face almost a complete napkin.
And yet no one has eaten. The water
Stays in the grass. A single blade
Stands to straighten its back, all the grass now
Like a runner wanting feeling in his legs and neck.
I'm sorry but the savages are savages. But to bring
Them nearer I'll say one of them, we don't
Like him, is just movement in the trees.

Back to the stream where there is a house with
A wall that has no purpose.
The house is burned out.
There is a chunk of fat and some flour on a table.

Merchants and sailors walk along white fences,
They are tall and there isn't any trembling in them.
Solitude isn't a gate that opens. Water stolen
Or borrowed. Solitude is being movement
In the trees, introduced and hated
As just movement in the trees. Our runner
Under a black crescent back to the village. The stream

By the house runs to the ocean. Our messenger runs
Because he knows the ways out of all places are of
Like distance. We arrive before him. He holds
His side.
There are fish in the stream. Rocks and a striped maple.
In the room below us
There is a chunk of fat and some flour on a table.
The discovery of the stream is important. Not to wash

Your face in it, but still to reconsider
Is all the meaning there is for you dropping the hoe
When you hear your wife join your older daughter screaming.
But leave it for the story. What will they be doing
At the ocean. Will they greet us. It will be by evening.

Fish from the stream, blue and orange,
Will wait quietly on a table to be cleaned.
Are we returning to morning? The scream
Empties into an ocean. That ocean.
Look to the left: five men, two of them fat,
In bright jackets are playing after supper,
That is they are doing artillery maneuvers
In dunes. Push and scratch.
A song goes up the stream. The fatter of the two falls
To his knees. His nose is bleeding.
Think of smoke, trees, or geese. We agree.
I've volunteered nothing to you. But this

Was peace.

II.

for my daughter

It bites through and then it opens wide, the white
Pimpernels are not out and then hiding, hiding
And indicated by redness and

Then again surprised inside, almost
All the flowers are now taken aside
To the little radiant corners where you have
Built a crude shelter with a sigh.

The lights are ganging up on us, two trees
Monopolize the season, with a stick
We draw a line and the sun crosses it before
It's finished. And then that night
It's cold. It begins. The last winter we get should
Adore us, holding and swinging
Our arms. The serfs
Kicking the straw high into the funny lights.
The pilgrims by now miss their suppers. Count sticks
In the walls. Good-bye, good-night.
Whether for the white pimpernels or not it's been
Like this: you roll to the right and close your eyes,
I walk outside and bite on a leaf
That survived this far. A young garter snake
Remembers what it was like yesterday and he divides
Everything you put inside his jar; everything outside,

And also captured.

III. PENNSYLVANIA, 1774

A young blond boy wakes suddenly, his eyes are
Bandaged, he stands with a gun and fires it,
Of all the other men sleeping around him no one is
Nudged, but hundreds of birds startled come up
All at once from the battlefield taking the sun

Twice away from him. A steward, saying *autumn*,
Twenty miles off is tossing a basin of water out
From a balcony. He hears the shot but will wait
To tell his wife about it at supper just at the point

That he first touches a spoon to his broth. He'll
Look up at her, there are wrinkles in the bowl,

Or on the pond behind their cottage. By the empty house.
I didn't tell you the blind soldier had shot *himself,*
Afraid that I would spoil
The steward's supper, but he did and it entered
At his shoulder. By now
He has bled to death, and the steward's wife is out
On the same balcony shouting
At her husband to come in off the pond
And wash himself. But the steward has drowned
Without a thought for any of us, and his wife

Is now dicing apples for her lieutenant who'll
Visit her in the morning. You are to imagine her walking
Back from the pond late that night through the tall
Grass, she's crying with her skirt over her face.
A leaf hits the pond. It's no disgrace that I have
Lived to finish this story.
We have walked the widow back to her cottage.

But we can't meet her son in the morning. (During
Their supper he shot himself in the shoulder.) No.
What was his father doing at that moment? Birds
Flying overhead. I'm sorry, but we've got this

All wrong and still it's over with.

IV.

So the little bird puts his chest up against us.
His chest

Goes from illusory to counterfeit. He decides
To confess: sure there is sadness

Climbing, don't be embarrassed if
You're caught feeding the donkey. He was

In love with it in sprouts. The colonies
Are twice gone. A runaway donkey

In a field with two barrels of molasses
On his back, the last exchanges

Of fraud like gunshots off behind the palisades.
They killed the donkey

For the heavy drums on his back; I know
The last few feet after he bought it,

He almost trotted across. He lost something.
I've been chased unbelievably

With the reluctance of importance and the steep
Aroma of a dead donkey who thought

Of himself differently at the very end.
You're not to think he poisoned the streams,

Everything decaying on his side, just all this
And one thought. A desire for alfalfa

And every legume. He almost trotted
Across. By degrees his rebellion sends us

The fresh monotony of repeating all this,
That it might be remembered, in the next century.

Might be remembered, and not us.

V.

Sweeping, sweeping. The leaves come off the trees
And you say to them: Listen, let's see you put
It all back on this minute. Everyone walks
Off to a secret place, a secret place which is
The first word of separation. The face of it is not
Inspiring, anyone crying anywhere.
It gets more and more difficult to listen.
The young lieutenant buttons his collar and says:

Listen, put it all back on this minute. The revolution
Of one young woman, her legs
Tucked under her, naked and crying on the bed.
The lieutenant storms out of the bedroom spilling
Something into another room. Outside a leaf
Slams up against her window. Most of your life
Your neck supports your head. Everything
Gets heavier. In the middle of the night in a lit room
The black cloth slips off the cage, and the canary
Bolts and begins singing to us his pure rumor
Of something not stupid or imaginary.

VI. PROSE: SCIRE FACIAS

How sadness defeats them. How thirty knights
Took their suppers still
On horses in their cold pavilion with women
Right and left spending light on them.
How sadness

Defeats them. The anxiety of a single leaf
Is visited on other leaves and just before
Something else up high, glowing and worried,
Came down and by to pass the night
Twice with a woman who eventually dies.

There is no importance to things that have
No importance. A romance. The dead bear
In a stream. Some movement in the trees.
A snake. And the deer, a cruel notary, loiters
With her signature.

The habit of saying this will break the fields
And wash between your toes. And then
Everything is concluded in heaven. I stepped
Out of the trees and told you how I had
Seen the massacre of a family. And then I
Went to eat. The next morning
I returned to the trees and really did see
A family taken individually and murdered.
I stepped back out of the trees and said
That today I had seen nothing worth mentioning
That you should believe.

But back in the pavilion a gigantic Saracen
Is eating a whole hen that has been boiled
In grape leaves. He will sleep
All night in a stream. The deer stands near him.

VII.

To have not long passed away we are accompanied
By ourselves. That is to say, not accompanied
At all, but more at the edge than we were,
Say, yesterday. That is, dead.
Six of them in black, their buckles tarnished,
Stand around our fire, or beside the grave.
They rub their hands together. In any event
They don't pray. They saved nothing
On a bone; even the bone is shaved
And plunged into the hair of a small girl
Who's washed her face and settled.

Each beginning is an intrusion on something
I've made. There was
Once a partner who sat down so many times
With me. And I just framed everything
In the nearest window. The snow came, a pond,
The settlers, tournaments, poor games,
And children puffing in the skins of beavers.
Erase the memory of the dead beaver, raw or
Pink, and steaming in the snow in daylight.

A young woman who's crossed an ocean is now
On her back, not in this landscape; her legs
Are up in the air, her hands hold on
To the railing behind her, blood leaves her knuckles,
Her mouth is saying something. You lean to
Hear it:

Put back your fears. Husband. Repose,
And a brown deer near a stone. Our children
Stand up in a clearing. They tell us
We didn't place ourselves. Look back
And the deer, in summary

Of all the economy of evening, has gone.

The Hour

for Camille

A dark, thick branch in the last light is like
The hand of your grandmother
Dropping linen napkins on the shrubs to dry
Hopelessly in the few hours before night.
Across the garden
In the back a girl strikes a piano key just once
And then there is the sound of crickets. The evening

Itself seems slow with the oldest feelings:
A boy walks up the hill
With a glass jar; inside he has, perhaps, a snake,
A firefly, or minnows. Three houses away
A man standing on his roof passes a short ladder
Down to his wife.

The stone nude beside the garden is bathing
In deep shade while inside the mouth
Of the nude in a copper dish a sparrow washes
Both its wings.

In the dark there's a last sound, it is
A large jar breaking in the street, and up into the night
Almost heavy
Go fireflies striking their soft, yellow lights.

A Village Priest

Washing the corpse, the boat, and her pine floors
Is better than the words I've kept in blame
Of the stairs and how she went down on her hip,
The tacking of female bone and a pin
With her memory of the room with yellow flowers:
She messed herself, she said, like the brains
Of a pumpkin. The seeds undigested, very white
And sweet. A dead old woman and my knife down
The sides of a boat, she loved the outline of herself
And touched it and followed it to the cove.

The wings of a snow-owl haven't an iron sound
But might if it had fallen asleep;
Margins of new snow like
A tree or a woman unfolding by a window in the morning.

She looks at me I think. I have been seen
By her twice like this and so now it's me who
Washes her corpse. The joints are mechanical and
Yet I test her still; the arm that worked the feather,
A poor student, is dropped and dropped.
The last bruise
Refusing to pull up like a smart bird now touches
The ground briefly and the legs of the mouse still
Working, half eaten; the small mouth eating altitude
For the first time. I have walked out of

The house and keep walking with a basin of used water
That must be thrown out.
Someone running away from a meteor stone and telling
Me afterward that it was only the snow-owl
Making his rounds, done for and somehow crumpled
On the ground.

She did it before with embarrassment, down the inside
Of her leg; he was always climbing the rocks, she washed
With wet beach sand. She was sorry for him for he certainly
Went back to the house and stood before a basin
With his genitals in one hand and with the other flinging
Water around.
The little bath of wet sand was with her like the lightning
That night which she described as frail
And living in the straw like mice.

She would say the cows are bedding down
In the field. It will rain.
The leaves are showing their undersides
By the pond. She smiled at me often.
And she would carry a bottle of kerosene to her side.
Her breasts have white centers while the eyes
Of the snow-owl
Revolve twice and then shut before flight.

Descent into the Hours of the Peregrine

A wet umbrella is open in the tub. It's midnight.
A paper airplane leaves his black room,
Dips in the hall and then plunges down through
The empty stairwell.

Everyone is asleep in the house except
For this small boy smiling from the center of his room.
He launched something light and fragile that the cat
Is now attacking downstairs: knocking it back
Into the air and then up against a wall.

There was a dead quiet in the house, and suddenly
A white paper airship entered the scene that included
Even a mother and father who are sleeping; something
Made a short pass through their house:
The boy knows it wasn't a bird or ghost
But something more lovable to a world of children

Like a charging bull elephant, white air
Streaming from the corners of its mouth.

The Pennacesse Leper Colony for Women, Cape Cod: 1922

for Laura

The island, you mustn't say, had only rocks and scrub pine;
Was on a blue, bright day like a blemish in this landscape.
And Charlotte who is frail and the youngest of us collects
Sticks and branches to start our fires, cries as they burn
Because they resemble most what she has lost
Or has little of: long fingers, her toes,
And a left arm gone past the elbow, soon clear to her shoulder.
She has the mouth of sea perch. Five of our sisters wear
Green hoods. You are touched by all of this, *but not by us.*
To be touched by us, to be kissed! Sometimes
We see couples rowing in the distance in yellow coats.

Sometimes they fish with handlines; we offend
Everyone who is offended most
And by everything and everyone. The five goats love us, though,
And live in our dark houses. When they are
Full with milk they climb the steps and beg that
They be milked. Their teats brush the steps and leave thick
Yellow trails of fresh milk. We are all females here.
Even the ghosts. We must wash, of course, in salt water,
But it smarts or maybe it even hurts us. Often with a rope
Around her waist Anne is lowered entirely into the water.
She splashes around and screams in pain. Her screams
Sometimes carry clear to the beaches on the Cape.

For us I say so often. For us we say. *For us!* We are
Human and not individual, we hold everything in common.
We are individual, you could pick us out in a crowd.
You did. This island is not our prison. We are not kept
In; not even by our skin.

Once Anne said she would love to be a Negro or a trout.

We live without you. Father, I don't know why I have written
You all this; but be proud for I am living, and yet each day
I am less and less your flesh. Someday, eventually, you
Should only think of me as being a lightning bug on the lawn,
Or the Negro fishing at the pond, or the fat trout he wraps
In leaves that he is showing to someone. I'll be

Most everything for you. And I'll be gone.

Pastoral

It happened so fast. Fenya was in the straight
Chair in the corner, her youngest sucking
On her breast. The screams, and a horseman
Outside the cottage. Then, her father in a blue tunic
Falling through the door onto the boards.
Fenya leaned over him, her blouse
Still at the waist and a single drop of her yellow milk
Falling into the open eye of her father. He dies
Looking up through this screen. What he sees

Is a little lampglow,
Like the poet describes less often even than harness bells
Or the icon with pine boughs. He sees snow
Falling into a bland field where a horse is giving
Birth to more snow, dragging its placenta all over
The glaze which is red; all the snow is red, the horse's
Blood is white. He sees tears on Fenya's face and
Milk coming like bone hairpins from her breasts.
The straight force in the twig that makes a great black
Branch. Two of which are crossed over his chest. Terror is

The vigil of astonishment.

The Obscure

It's the poor first light of morning.

The woman still sleeps in her unheated room.
The man in his nightshirt stands
In the kitchen burning
Dry sunflower stalks in the open stove.
There's not a single lamp working.
The orange light from the stove
Shows just the things in the far corner.

Outside the window it is still snowing.

The harvest is finished. The time has come
For killing the pig.
They have been starving him for a week;
Yesterday, emptying him completely
With a wet portion of barley meal.
The pig is hungry and squeals in his corner
By the garden.

The man has dressed in an old canvas coat.
He stands inside the branch fence
Beside the sty, and with a broom sweeps
A clearing in the snow.
He lays out the knives, the rope,
And a black stool.

Birds stream from the tree above him.

The pig is stuck in the windpipe, he hangs
By the rope from the tree, and upside down
Spins slowly above the stool,

His eyes never leave this man
Who brought him so many warm vegetables.

The man's thoughts never leave the woman
Who is still sleeping up in the house.
She walked through the woods in the snow
For most of the evening. For the second night
In their lives she wouldn't be touched
By him.

The pig is ready for scalding. He has
Never before been this heated and pink.
A high window opens in the house. Icicles fall
From the windowsill. The woman looks out
Opening her eyes to the bright snow:
The pig hangs in the tree like an ornament of wax
Stuck with a few red jewels — she had not
Been warned about the killing;
There's her scream and then
Just a silence leaving the man to himself,

To little else but the thought
That her breasts filled the window like a mouth.

About Infinity

after H.H., The 17th Karmapa

There are stonebreakers in straw hats
Drinking from jars under a shade tree.
You are dressed all in white like the clematis
And look down into a meadow where your father
Is working on a watercolor of two silver trees.
The two trees are parallel.
He looks back at you:
You are wishing he hadn't died making with
His chest a sound like cows running in a stream.

Cows eat the flowers, they eat off the trees;
And the seed packets of the milk-white clematis
Have no turnings: they sit, almost purple,
In steady needles that are vertical, North
And South, repeating abstractly
That such parallel things must meet
Somewhere in a limitless glut of peace.

There are men in straw hats drinking from clear
Jars of water.
There are two silver trees whose pink roots
Will meet, not abstractly, but under the meadow
Where for minerals and the water
They mean to kill each other. There are cows

Running in a running stream.

Anima Poeta: A Christmas Entry for the Suicide, Mayakovsky

It has nothing to do with the warmth of moonset
If I say to you
The cities are prose, or that my daughter
Is growing more beautiful than
Before when her hair was white and cut short.
The first Wednesday after the peace
With Germany was like a new brook
Under the rain, which only the rain could make.

You dream of a steamer with a clean pine cabin.
The fog in the wreaths.
The bullets were chalk-white larvae
That slept in the chambers
Of a revolver you left near the door;
Larvae, a Latin word for ghosts,
The pieces of iron letting go
Of their little red hammer and its stirrup
Sending you a visitor,
The moth that dips inside your head: you were
Gone before you hit the boards of the floor

Think of yourself with your black fingers
In the flowerpots, in the candlelight,
The double violets and scarlet Anthus
Of a narrow window.
You were trying
To remember the French word
For a hedgerow sparrow that soldiers
Made captive for its song. You thought
The kingfisher
Was so slow when in the vicinity of winter
That even a bureaucrat

Would distinguish all its colors. Mayakovsky,
You watched a snail one afternoon eat twice
Its length in brooklime.
When you were young

You could list all the birds of passage;
Much later in your life you joined them.

Monologue of Two Moons, Nudes with Crests: 1938

for Francesca

Once, Lily and I fell from a ladder
And startled the white geese that were
Concealed in the shadows of the house, and
I wrote much later that the geese
Broke from the shadows like handkerchiefs
Out of the sleeves of black dresses

At a burial. When the matron was sick
It was work to carry the powders
On blue paper and the clear water
With a spoon into her large, cold room.

In the evenings we would look out
At the spruce trees. It was wrong to have
Visitors. It was wrong those clear nights
To remember that boys were out on the hills
Falling onto sleds or into their gray baskets.

We were two young girls with black hair
And the white cones
Of our breasts. Lily said, "I will put
My hand, here, on you and follow the rib, and
You can put your hand, here, on me,
Up the inside of my leg."
We spent that Christmas morning pressing
Satin skirts for the boys' choir. We take
Butter away from the closet.
We take the lamp away from the green
Cadaverous child who is not ours.

I have a little violin pupil who eats
Bread in cream.

We love the details mice leave in flour.
The way the clouds
Are low before a storm in early summer.

Lily slept with a Jew once in Vienna.
I opened my hand that morning
On a milk jug that had frozen and cracked
On the doorstep.
Yesterday, I saw the perfect impression
Of a bee in asphalt. It was under a shade tree.
Lily said, "I will kiss in the morning
Your mouth which will be red and thick
After sleep." She has left me
For a banker she met in the gardens.
The gas jets are on: they are
Like fountains of the best water. I am

Remembering the vertical action of two birds
Building a nest. It's in Munich and
Both birds are dark and crested,
But the female, I think, is the one whose
Nesting materials are wet things:

Twigs, leaves, and an infinite black string.

Elegy Asking That It Be the Last

for Ingrid Erhardt, 1951–1971

There's a bird the color of mustard. The bird
Is held in a black glove. This bird
Has a worm in its heart.
Inside the heart of the worm there's
A green passage of blood.
The bird is a linnet.
The glove is worn by a Prince. There's a horse
Under him. It is another century: things are
Not better or worse. The horse is chestnut,
The horse
Is moving its bowels while standing in the surf.
The cliffs behind him are dark. It is
The coast of Scotland. It's winter.
Surrounding the Prince and also on horses are men
Who are giant; they are dressed in furs.
There's ice forming in their beards. Each is
A chieftain. They are the Prince's heavy protection.
They are drunk, these men who are laughing
At the linnet with a worm in its heart.
This is a world set apart from ours. It is not!

Nineteen Forty

They got Lewes at last yesterday.
VIRGINIA WOOLF

The sun just drops down through the poplars.

I should sit out and watch it rather than
Write this!

The red of it sweeps along the houses past the marsh
To where L. is picking apples.
The air is cold.
Little things seem large.
Behind me there's moisture like windows on the pears.

And then the planes going to London. Well, it's
An hour before that yet. There are cows eating grass.
There were bombs dropped on Itford Hill. Yesterday,
I watched a Messerschmitt smudge out in the sky.

What is it like when the bone-shade is crushed in
On your eye. You drain. And pant. And, then, dot, dot, dot!

Walking Sunday (Natalie's birthday) by Kingfisher Pool
I saw my first hospital train. It was slow but not laden,
Not like a black shoebox but like a weight pulled by
A string. And bone-shaking!
Private and heavy it cut through the yellow fields:

And a young airman with his head in his hands,
With his head in a fat, soiled bandage, moved
His good eye, and nothing else, up to the high corner
Of his window and through the cool, tinted glass watched,

I believe, as
Individual wild ducks scraped and screamed in along a marsh.

February: The Boy Brueghel

The birches stand in their beggar's row:
Each poor tree
Has had its wrists nearly
Torn from the clear sleeves of bone,
These icy trees
Are hanging by their thumbs
Under a sun
That will begin to heal them soon,
Each will climb out
Of its own blue, oval mouth;
The river groans,
Two birds call out from the woods

And a fox crosses through snow
Down a hill; then, he runs,
He has overcome something white
Beside a white bush, he shakes
It twice, and as he turns
For the woods, the blood on the snow

Looks like the red fox,
At a distance, running down the hill:
A white rabbit in his mouth killed
By the fox in snow
Is killed over and over as just
Two colors, now, on a winter hill:

Two colors! Red and white. A barber's bowl!
Two colors like the peppers
In the windows
Of the town below the hill. Smoke comes
From the chimneys. Everything is still.

Ice in the river begins to move,
And a boy in a red shirt who woke
A moment ago
Watches from his window
The street where an ox
Who's broken out of his hut
Stands in the fresh snow
Staring cross-eyed at the boy
Who smiles and looks out
Across the roof to the hill;
And the sun is reaching down
Into the woods

Where the smoky red fox still
Eats his kill. Two colors.
Just two colors!
A sunrise. The snow.

The Czar's Last Christmas Letter:
A Barn in the Urals

for Robert

You were never told, Mother, how old Illya was drunk
That last holiday, for five days and nights

He stumbled through Petersburg forming
A choir of mutes, he dressed them in pink ascension gowns

And, then, sold Father's Tirietz stallion so to rent
A hall for his Christmas recital: the audience

Was rowdy but Illya in his black robes turned on them
And gave them that look of his; the hall fell silent

And violently he threw his hair to the side and up
Went the baton — the recital ended exactly one hour

Later when Illya suddenly turned and bowed
And his mutes bowed, and what applause and hollering

Followed.
All of his cronies were there!

Illya told us later that he thought the voices
Of mutes combine in a sound

Like wind passing through big, winter pines.
Mother, if for no other reason I regret the war

With Japan for, you must now be told,
It took the servant, Illya, from us. *It was confirmed.*

He would sit on the rocks by the water and with his stiletto
Open clams and pop the raw meats into his mouth

And drool and laugh at us children.
We hear guns often, now, down near the village.

Don't think me a coward, Mother, but it is comfortable
Now that I am no longer Czar. I can take pleasure

From just a cup of clear water. I hear Illya's choir often.
I teach the children about decreasing fractions, that is

A lesson best taught by the father.
Alexandra conducts the French and singing lessons.

Mother, we are again a physical couple.
I brush out her hair for her at night.

She thinks that we'll be rowing outside Geneva
By the Spring. I hope she won't be disappointed.

Yesterday morning while bread was frying
In one corner, she in another washed all of her legs

Right in front of the children. I think
We became sad at her beauty. She has a purple bruise

On an ankle.
Like Illya I made her chew on mint.

Our Christmas will be in this excellent barn.
The guards flirt with your granddaughters and I see...

I see nothing wrong with it. Your little one, who is
Now a woman, made one soldier pose for her; she did

Him in charcoal, but as a bold nude. He was
Such an obvious virgin about it; he was wonderful!

Today, that same young man found us an enormous azure
And pearl samovar. Once, he called me Great Father

And got confused.
He refused to let me touch him.

I know they keep your letters from us. But, Mother,
The day they finally put them in my hands

I'll know that possessing them I am condemned
And possibly even my wife, and my children?

We will drink mint tea this evening.
Will each of us be increased by death?

With fractions as the bottom integer gets bigger, Mother, it
Represents less. That's the feeling I have about

This letter. I am at your request, The Czar.
And I am Nicholas.

These Untitled Little Verses in Which, at Dawn, Two Obscure Dutch Peasants Struggled with an Auburn Horse

The water is green. The two boats out at a distance
Are silver, and the two gulls coming in

Off the water are, also, silver;
But these peasants and their horse, at first light,

Seem absorbed in the pitch-blackness
Of a previous night. They are in a field

That climbs away from the sea joining
A thick row of white almond trees.

The younger of the two men holds a small branch,
The other

Holds a rope that leads away from the horse
Running over his shoulder and underneath the arm

To a pool of rope beneath him: he leans,
Or he reclines like a lever in the scene.

The auburn horse
Represents some inevitable sadness

That will visit each of us, that visits
These two peasants struggling in a winter pasture.

It is the morning.
It is dawn. These three may

Signal a common enough passage from the night
To the day. It begins like pain for the older man:

It begins to rain.
The two men run to the trees just above them

And the horse, ignorant of everything, walks away
Like a skilled butcher from a dark, maimed

Lamb still wiggling in the grass behind him. And
Morning surrenders to midday, and the afternoon

To the evening, and the evening surrenders everything
To the sleep of these two peasants

Who have had a discouraging day in the fields:
They dream of the black, burial horses of a king

With heavy sable plumes and the blinders
Of gold-leaf made starry with diamonds,

Horses not like the auburn mare who stood
In a world that

Belongs to a system of things
Which presents a dark humus with everything

Living: all of us preceded
Not by the lovely, braided horses

Of which the peasants dreamed, but by these two
Peasants and their horse struggling

Briefly, at dawn, in the deep trenches
Of a field beside the green, winter sea.

Her Monologue of Dark Crepe
with Edges of Light:

Mistress Adrienne, I have been given a bed with a pink dresser
In the hothouse
Joining the Concord Public Library: the walls and roof are
Glass and my privacy comes from the apple-geraniums,
Violets, ferns, marigolds, and white mayflags.
I get my meals
With the janitor and his wife and all of the books are mine
To use. I scour, sweep, and dust.
I hope you don't think of me
As a runaway? I remember your kindness,
Your lessons in reading and writing on the piazza.
My journey was unusual. I saw some of the war
And it was terrible even far up into the North.
My first fright was at a train depot outside Memphis
Where some soldiers found me eating not yet ripened
Quinces and grapes, they took me prisoner: first
I helped some children carry tree limbs to the woodbox
Of the locomotive, then, I was shown to a gentleman
In the passenger car who was searching for his runaway
Negress in a purple dress; he wouldn't identify me,

And I was thrown in with about forty stray blacks into
An open boxcar and soon we were moving, next to me
A man was sucking on the small breasts of a girl
Maybe twelve years of age, across from them
A sad old woman smiled as she puffed on an old cigar end,
By afternoon she was dead, her two friends
Just kicked her out so that she rolled down into pasture
Frightening some hogs that ran off into a thicket.
The girl next to me whimpered and shook. Those quinces
Just ran straight through me and all I could do was
Squat in one corner that was supplied with ammonia-waters

And hay. We were given that night Confederate uniforms
To mend and when the others slept I dressed in three
Shirts and trousers and leapt from the moving train,
The padding helped some but I couldn't walk the next day.
I hid in a shack that seemed lonely but for a flock
Of turkeys, some young hens, and a corncrib with tall
Split palings. The next morning from a hill
I watched field-workers on a tobacco plantation, it took
Two men to carry a single leaf like a corpse from
A battle scene. That night I found a horse with a bit
In its mouth made of telegraph wire. He carried me up all
The way to Youngstown. *Chloe, you must
Learn to swim in the pond and to ride the old sorrel.*
I am grateful. I had to swim two rivers. I fished some
For perch, bream, and trout and ate dried berries.
I stole a bushel of oysters from the porch of a farmhouse.
I treated my sores with blackgum from poplars. I witnessed
The hanging of three Confederate soldiers at a trestle:
Once they were done dancing, they settled in their greatcoats
Like dead folded birds. I have a hatred
Of men and I walked away from the trestle singing.
I spoke to The Concord Literary Club last Tuesday
About my experiences. I told them you never did
Abuse me. How we would sit out in the gazebo
And listen to the boys with their violins, tambourines,
Bones, drums and sticks. How we wept as girls
When the fox bit the head off our peahen and that
From that day how the peacock, missing his mate, would
See her in his reflection in a downstairs window
And fly at it increasing his iridescence with lacerations.
When I left you the windows were all missing and daubers
Were making their mud houses in the high corners
Of the hallway. With sugar-water and crepe I have put a new
Hem on my purple dress.

At night I walk down the aisles
Of the library, the books climb twenty feet above me,

I just walk there naked with my tiny lamp.
I have the need to fling the lamp sometimes: but I resist it.
Mistress Adrienne, I saw three big cities burning!
Did you know ladies from Philadelphia rode for two days
In wagons to climb a hill where with spyglasses they watched
The war like a horse-pulling contest at a fair.
The man beside me on the train who was sucking the little
Girl's breasts, he was your stable boy, Napoleon. He said
He never had a bad word for you. His little mistress was
Still bare to the waist and before I leapt from the train,
And while he slept, I ran a rod into his eye. I stabbed him
In his brain. She stopped weeping.
Remember that French lullaby where two fleas in a gentleman's
Mustache die like a kiss between the lips of the gentleman
And his mistress. How we laughed at it!
I hope you were not long unconscious there beside the pond.
I just ran away from you, listening the whole night
For your father's hounds. I am
Afraid I split your parasol on your skull. If I
Don't hear from you I will try to understand. *Chloe.*

The Wedding Party

for Marianne

When the large frame of the window collapses in the fire
It's like a huge woman
With her hands on her hips, the bones below her waist
Spread with leaves, about to strike
A frail child and the bones of his face
Spread with more leaves, two
Bowls slapped with mud and baked with everyone outside
Screaming in the smoke in the hall where she waltzed
Away, she thought, with the sergeant.

There are phrases like cold fish, or a triangle balanced
On the nose of another triangle. The woman in a formal gown
Tossed out on the snow, a black leg and her husband draped
Over the table with his hand in the punch bowl. The daughter
Was near the folded chair in the middle of the wall.

But don't stop; cross the room and follow those people
Just coming in; go down the stairs
Leading to the toilets;
Open the door in front of you; the small cellar
With the window kicked out. It will all come down
To this level. The barrel organs, the hat that collected
The printed invitations, the conductor, the vows,
And the bean flower the bride had grown for her father.

These are not the memories of a country wedding.
The one bird brought inside appears outside
And will not be interviewed.
Even the amateurs who moved the piano
Have gone aside with their sandwiches. Their boss takes
Off his spectacles, lays them down, gazes beyond
It all at some addition to the moon. You must look

At her as well. He decides whether or not to take off
His hat. To drink? *Can you hear me? Just yes or no.*

The women huddled on the roof far away are disappointed;
The thrill, the calamity, was over.
Hadn't it just started? They hug their blankets.
One by one they climb down the ladder in boredom.
Getting into bed the second time within
Two hours is a dilemma not like dying in a fire after
The wedding. And
In the extreme heat the tuba in the corner took on
A new curl. In the morning a small boy blows into it.
A drunk lying out in the trees hears him,
All the false starts, nothing like it in the world. The music
Telling him to get up and walk away. But first he searches
For the hat that he wore to a wedding.

The Immoralist

Samaden, the Julier, Tiefenkasten... the raw egg
I broke into the harness bells, and the strong reversals
Of cold, sour wine. The marshlike waters on the other
Honeymoon were a new train, as early as Neuchâtel, and
Overlooking a lake, past some cows, the first signals
Of melancholy. I didn't leave her all day.

I had heard of other cases of tuberculosis
That were much worse. And wasn't there something
I didn't know about myself? I blamed everything on
Whatever few biscuits Marceline broke
Into her soup. She coughed horribly.
Besides, what did we need money for? A winter in Engadine?
I no longer have my lectures. We are drunk and weak.

I have again made love to a woman saving blood
In her mouth. I remember the way the other sloshed
Wine around with her tongue. Her laughter.
And the reeds of a hideous black lake. The hotel
Was empty. The honest Swiss. Even their rosebushes
Told her I would push a pillow
To her face. (Hard benches by the water, and the blankets
Over her legs. I didn't leave her all day.)

From the train through glass: larches and fir,
And the crease of the pillowcase on her black cheek
Filling slowly like her grave,
Like the trench of a young couple crossing a lake.

Sun and Moon Flowers: Paul Klee, 1879–1940

First, there is the memory of the dead priest in Norway
Dressed in a straw hat, his tie that's white
But splashed with violet, and the black skirt;
He'll hang forever in the deer park.
Beneath him German officers
Are weaving in and out of trees in a white sunlight.

When there is music crossing over the water from France
The little steamers pull their beds of coal
Slowly up the canal, and, Klee,
You walk back to your room saying,
"What on earth happened to us? Any simple loss
Is like the loss of all of us. Nothing's secret?
Just look straight into the North Sea.
And, then, tell me there's anything they can keep from us."

The matron who walked you through the orchard at Orsolina
Should have said, "There's a black star with conifers."
Klee, don't listen to them. Next Wednesday your heart
Stops like a toad. You're dying of a skin disease.
They are not telling you about this war, the Luftwaffe,
The Nazi who's resting on a sofa beside a stream
And, Klee, this Nazi is inside Poland. And,
In Poland your moon flowers have already begun growing!

The opaque dice in your painting can no longer
Be mistaken for some weathered houses by the coast.
The woman sick with tuberculosis says to you,
"A war will clear the air!"
The war puts priests in trees. Puts a sparrow's nest
Beside a sleeve in a train station in Tuscany.
You and your friends saw the unlikely, ruptured ceilings
And painted them; but not as premonitions, or images

Of war—
The war your family won't acknowledge or discuss
But an orderly who has news of Poland whispers
To the day nurse: she touches her blouse.
You ask her what is happening.
You make a scene. And then she says what is necessary
By slipping you a morning tray

With its ice water, blue spikes of lupine, and morphine.

Ibis

for Lori Goldensohn

There is the long dream in the afternoon
That turns a large, white page

Like, once, the slow movement
Of slaves at daybreak

Through the clouds of a stone laundry.
The blossom

On a black vegetable and
The olive wood burning in the plate

Are the simple events
That I'll wake to this evening.

At dark, we'll walk out along
The shore having finished

Another day of exile in a wet place.
As a boy I burned

Leaves in the many gardens
Of a cemetery in Rome.

I wrote in my diary:
A blue vessel

Is filling out in the rain. All day,
Here, the water falls and is not broken,

But it punishes me like the girls
With their clubs and bowl

Flattening the new maize,
Millet, and the narrow tubers

Of yam
That are white like hill snow.

Postumius is my servant-boy, he plays
All morning in the sea.

He says, "Ovid. The red ibis flies north!"
I hate him.

He visits me between phantoms
And like them,

Like the goat, you can trace the muscles
In his leg and the purple ropes

Of blood that climb
Through his throat. At the salt marsh

He searches for the moon snail
With its lavender egg-pouch;

He eats them after
Soaking them in brookwater...

Days that follow in rain
Make him nervous and he eats

Everything off the dry shelf: the individual
Oval seeds, he cracks

The winter wheat between his teeth
With a sound

Like a child working its teeth
In a bad dream.

If he stands all day in the marsh
In the sun, then, he returns to me

As a new coin. I am jealous
Of him.

He smiles at me. There are the shadows
With the olive wood burning in the plate.

It's dark. We walk out along
The shore of the Black Sea.

There's the noise of the ibis
Who raises a bleached wing in waking.

There is a boat decaying by a tree.
It's radiant

Like the shearwater birds
Standing here and there among rocks.

Postumius touches my shoulder, "Ovid?
About Rome when the moon

Was broken on the ground and the ferns
Stood against the blue-black sky?"

I do remember the bleachers in the arena
And a lion's paw raised, that erased

The face of a young Thracian.
I tell him he is a stupid boy!

We walk back
Passing the wharves and straw-houses.

I say to Postumius
That when I am dead

He must fuel the terra-cotta lamp
And gather the cress and hidden eggs

Of the ibis. He smiles at me, I do
Love him, at moments;

As, then, he sleeps next to me,
Never sharing the work

Of turning the page, as slowly he turns
All of his new body away from me.

The Trees of Madame Blavatsky

for my sister

There is always the cough. In the afternoon
They go out for long walks as partners,
Arms linked, woman and woman,
Man and man, woman and man. And they keep
Their feet. I can't judge if she supports
The other in green.
Perhaps, they support each other? I've
Followed them for miles and they conceal
Everything in weakness. They have
The hind legs of cows.
When horses eat fermented hay it brings up
The lining of the intestine which they
Tug at
Like gloves all the way past the elbows.

If we could follow them far enough we would
Come to their meeting place
Where they are all wired up like flowers:
They live in this camp, serene and delayed.
They are the oldest sopranos resuming
With care the phrases,
Listen, there is a song they sing at night,
The regalia inside their chests, and this song,
Which blames the memory, is wrong and not wrong
Like a girl
Showing her breasts to a boy in a cemetery.

The Moths

for my mother

I. CIRCA 1582

The peninsula seen from the hills near Bath
Was a sullen black orchis, its back almost broken,
And a wooden ship once went down the river
And sat just past the headwaters at Popham,

And men, women with children, dopper birds, cows,
And sheep walked out onto the sand,
Behind them the topsheets and sails were collapsing:
A great foresail followed by darkening mists

And white clews moving with mainsail
And an old sun dropping with the wet spanker.
These settlers with coughing and diarrhea
Just walked across the beach into the woods.

They made a clearing where moose would come
To eat pole-beans and lettuce.
Protestant carpenters making windowframes; and
By winter, sucking on salep and safflower, they will

Be rubbing coffins with the gestures of skaters.
A girl looks out through the trees
Remembering her fen-runners, the wax shoes
Used as skates when the gray, low-country moors were

Frozen. She remembers how the tiny oaks were silver
And blue in the snow; she'll soon be a pale, steaming
Nude in the outer lodge beside the pines
And she'll be mostly blue except for the red sores.

The Smiths, Hamels, and the Ewbanks returned
To the ship in February
And the rest of their company were left in the lodge
Unburied to spindle and fray in the first hot days

Of April. Just Littre's-glands, coughing, and diarrhea:
All through March the survivors would walk
Out along the deck and every so often there was a quick
Twist of the neck, a nervous look at the beach

Where ghosts appeared like a crazy, pearl bobbin jumping
On a nail of bone.
They remembered the green manure in their barns. Their
Dead were imagined in this fen-landscape.

Luke's cheeks were like two steady roses!
The wind stopped, and the river gave up the boat
Like a ghost with its topsails, studding sails, and clews.
At first the woods smelled bad like an old shoe.

But then large gulls began appearing at windows
In the outer lodge, and Lewis Hamel's magnifying-glass
Drew through it sunlight, and the straw and sulfur
Smoked, the flames consumed everything nearly down to

The old gardens. They had buried their dead with fire
While they were crossing the water:
The reality of wilderness as elopement
Like believing someone is most in when there is just

An empty bed and the orchard ladder reaching to
The window; then, finding her gone they say she's dead
When she's most alive, a new bride by morning. The girl
In the lodge had blotches on her cheeks like moths:

These are her mother's fingerprints left as she touched
Her daughter last, and the icy moths

Are also like some soft fossil of a shell
You might discover out walking in the woods

Where, once, there was a peaceful, tropical ocean.

II. CIRCA 1952

Indians stood on a hill in Bath and watched
The woods burn all afternoon, the dark smoke
Rising from the very point of the peninsula.
They believe that if you know everything

About your past you had better also know
The present moment; the risk
Isn't that you'll live in the past,
But there *and in a future*

That repeats the past. For the first time
In my life I am happy and
Living here in a desert. The palms
And lime trees have a fragrance in November

That I describe for friends in letters.
After twenty years I can now describe
The peninsula, how in April they could finally
Break the ground, and I went to Popham Village

With my father and there would be a half-dozen
Open graves and the fishermen and farmers
Who died in the winter were brought out of the Stone
House and put in the ground. Just

My father and I, a deacon and the diggers,
Hearing the prayer repeated. We would
Look out at the water and watch Morris Cobb
In his rowboat checking his lobster traps in the cove:

He is orderly like my father, now, moving from hole
To hole and, then,
I would realize his voice had fallen,
And my father moved in his robes, choking

As he moved. While other children wondered
What happened to the dead I would
Wonder what they did with the dirt
That a coffin displaces.

When the father dies you follow him to the grave
And then walk away without him. I followed my father
To the edge but then walked back with him
Talking about something unimportant. We learn

From pilgrims raising their great beige mainsail,
Braided royals, and the hard slamming clews.
They practically flew away in their wooden boat.
Ghostly, they put their backs to ghosts.

The iron buckles and sleeves on a sail look
Like the dead orange fronds
Up in the palms. The ground snails
Falling out of the palms when it rains are

An interior weather like rain
Mixed with ice up and down the coast, and my mother
And I bringing in the wash from outside
With everything gone stiff like boards.

She was a nurse on a surgical ward in the hospital
At Bath.
Some nights she would come back to us
And sit and look straight out the window

Past the trees to other trees.
In the winter fog you would try to sleep

And the foghorn at Small Point changed
The rhythm of your breathing. We lived in a seventeenth-

Century parsonage and it did creak. The doorstone had
Lichen that shaded the stone into a face
Like an old man wearing a night-bonnet.
The Blaisdales' grandfather insisted it was

Reverend Cotter who died in the house in his sleep.
He was poisoned by a housekeeper.
She hanged herself
Out in the stable. And it was Cotter who planted

The lilac hedge outside my bedroom window;
When the wind came down from Sebasco Estates
My mother would jam the window with a dictionary
And all the rooms of the old house filled

With the smell of snapped lilac. Moose sometimes
Chewed at it. Once I woke in the morning
To the slobbering head of a cow moose through the window.
And my father during the week is at school in Bangor.

And my mother pale with her red hair rests,
At midnight, looking out the kitchen window where
All summer the fat moths were knocking their
Brains out against the lamp in the henhouse,

But now the moths are replaced with large
Flakes of snow, and there's no difference, moths
Or snow, for their lives are so short
That while they live they are already historical

Like a woman who knows too much about
The day before, who knows herself too well
There at the window, and who sadly
Touches a child's blue waterglass

As the old standing-clock in the hall begins
To slow and climb, slower and slower,
Through a thousand gears and ratchets
Into what she knew best, and

Into tomorrow.

Elegies for the Ocher Deer on the Walls at Lascaux

This and the like together establish the realm of IT.
 *"In order to come to love," says Kierkegaard about his
renunciation of Regina Olsen, "I had to remove the object."
 Kierkegaard does not conceal from us for a moment
that his religious doctrine of loneliness is personal. He
confesses that he "ceased to have common speech" with
men. He notes that the finest moment in his life is in the
bathhouse, before he plunges into the water: "by then I
am having nothing more to do with the world."*

MARTIN BUBER

PROLOGUE

You are hearing a distant, almost familiar, French cradlesong
While drinking bottled water
Along the roadside to Copenhagen.

There are children of six who speak
In secret to imaginary friends
On summer evenings before bed.

In some old houses there are walls where there were doors.
And doors where there were windows.
And where there were once floors of broken fieldstones
There are, now, blue ceilings.

There is a sudden smell of roses in a room.

Once, there was a hunter
Dressed in skins, in the black and mauve summer-molt of bison,
And he would squat down before a wet, serpentine wall and make
An image. (A virgin is singing, *My Lords, turn in, turn in!*)

I suppose all of this means nothing to you; there's still
The blue tiles of the bathhouse floor, and the orange lamps
Burning above the moving surface of the water. A nude lawyer
Is smoking a cigar on a birch-sofa next to a lieutenant
Who's exercising in an army blanket. You'll forget them
As you leave the edge making a little figure
In the air as you enter the steaming, blue pool:

Søren, a winter evening in the bathhouse, and just past
The surface of the water you saw
The *will to be!*

The *will to be* is, perhaps, teeth, throat,
And intestine leaving the floor of an ocean
With the slight movement of its tail. The *will to be* is often
Not pretty, but dorsal like the sable plumes on helmets, or

Like the man at Lascaux in his black-and-mauve skins
Who with friends stands at the edge of a pit
That holds reindeer, they shower the deer with stones,
And, then, there's a silence: our caveman

Reaches down into the pit and draws out a white fawn
Who, weak from swimming in the blood of the others, wobbles
For a moment and, then, runs off into a forest: *and, Søren,*

The fawn made bright, finite tracks through the leaves
Like your own red lettering in a diary

That believes the gods of China must be Chinese.

I. 1916

The way the mist in the mountains can circle a young fir,
A boulder, or the fern and purple vetch of the timberline
Which are waving as children after a pageant

Through the mist and rain to someone seated way above them
On a rotting bench at the summit of the mountain.
It's young Theodisius, the Jesuit,

Breathing heavily
After his climb, remembering a formal procession
Up a hill in St. Louis. He looks down through the Notch:

The priest knows desire to be a comedy of place and
A surge forward as with the boy and his tuba
In this parade at St. Louis: the boy had become faint
In his blue wool suit and silver cap,
And so under the sun while descending the hill he suddenly
Went rudely through ranks of clarinets and, then,
He wrecked a section of oboes and bassoons:

Death is a descent, or the traverse that is like
A surprising destruction of music moving
With the force of a sunstruck tuba
Down a hill where, at last, our fainting musician falls
Into the arms of laughing women
Who are wearing large hats and red pantaloons.

Theodisius is romantic; he has climbed a mountain
In the mist and rain to wait, now, through the day
For a change in the weather, for the sun to burn through
And what joy he'll feel

At the ease with which individual trees
Are regained in a familiar enough
Landscape of mountains with a clear lake and ponds.

In China, Theodisius would be mistaken for an eccentric,

But a conventional Chinese wisdom has always taken
The musician in his green trout-gown for being

Eccentric as he is musical.
Theodisius's instrument was the tuba.

Yes, our Jesuit often thinks of concepts of death
When reminded of childhood embarrassments.
Theodisius is a young Jesuit who remembers
The sad little crèche in Bethlehem.

He is now waiting for the sun to burn away the mist
In the mountains: *the beer gardens of St. Louis were often
Like this.* Anyway,

The fern and purple vetch are waving to the young priest
Who leaves his wet bench like Odysseus climbing up
Out of the surf: it's early morning,
He stares to the east where he thinks the sun will soon
Break everything wide open:

Theodisius, our poor Theodisius, still stands in mist.

He studies the cascades and a flaw in an icy waterfall,
He remembers
How his mother each spring boiled her best crystal chandelier
Through the long hours of the afternoon into evening.
Theodisius believes that beyond all doubt he is dangerous
To himself.

There have been many changes in him, and none
In the weather: he remembers
His mother's playing cards that were perfumed with balsam,
And how confidently she flicked them out singly

Over the table, how the young men seated
At the table could not remove their eyes
From her quick hands or her exposed bosom just beyond them.

Once crossing a stream with her, here, in these mountains
She lifted her skirts like the women in the lithograph
Of a circus at Trieste,
And Theodisius, a boy of twelve, went face first
Into the water, his mother laughing as she joined him:

They are both laughing now as they embrace,
Suspended, not quite seated on the streambed.
Theodisius thought all the colors of that lithograph
Were there in that water. He forgets,

And looks down into the spruce and aspen.
He spots several deer along the edges of a clearing.
He approaches them like a man
Falling through crust in a snowfield.
He is still thinking of his mother; this time, as she leans
Smiling over a balcony beside a white tree.
He thought the skin of the deer seemed shaded
As with lichen. The deer knew he was weak.
But they clattered off over the stone surface of the clearing
Into the mist and leaves.
Theodisius looked away from them to the running stream
With its small delays: the silver archipelagoes,

Pools and blue basins.
He remembered Greek girls dancing in the beer gardens
Of St. Louis.

Deserted even by the gentle deer, Theodisius

Became monumental and literal: he believed
He was the breeze tipping a wet bough of a tree, a breeze
Created by the passing of a red caboose pulled along swiftly
Over a mountain trellis,

A mountain trellis which stands in the sudden sunlight
Just beneath him, the mountain trellis

From which he hangs by the neck like the pastel daredevil
At Trieste in a famous lithograph
His mother nailed to the headboard of his small bed

Just beneath a chartreuse and red watercolor of the dead Jesus.

II. 1872

Isiah Potter walks solemnly from his old saltbox
And tar-shingle house onto the stone walk
And looks up the street past the roses
To the granite hitching posts. He loves the Orient.

Reverend Potter is composing a sermon
On the tragedy of green. He walks down the street
Under the elms thinking that once in a vision
He saw two men mowing in a field: there were ashes
On their shoulders and long daffodils shot through
Their necks and chests like arrows: he heard

An isolated choir up in a stand of trees
Behind the field. He woke, it was midnight
And he went down to the kitchen for bread in milk.
His father, Amos,
Had been dead for two winters. All the new moons
And Sabbaths. The grief calling of women and children.
Isiah Potter killed himself by leaping
From a ledge into the lake. The village wanted
A dull lighting of his face, a green abscissa
In his memory, in the vestibule of the meetinghouse.
The portrait of Isiah Potter has remained
In the vestibule for a hundred years, and

The nighthawks are still crying above the ledges of the lake,
And below them on the rocks a young raccoon
Who's eaten a sunfish washes his paws
And legs; he looks up at the night sky where

Suddenly there is something like sheet lightning
Giving way to the yellow, blue, and pink parachutes
Of The Chinese Fire & Rain which is spreading out
Over the lake and dissolving back into a white light,
And, again, it's the arsenic and antimony
Of The Snow Orchard: this is fireworks

Streaming steadily, now, from two large wooden boats
That were rowed quietly to the middle of the lake.

There's the shooting sparks of The Blue Fox.
The Snow Orchard, again, but mixed with two rockets
Of gold Cassandra Buttons, and, then, after a silence
Where the frogs begin once more with their groaning:
There's the explosion of a loud, red Camphor Goose.

There's the smell of gunpowder. You can hear the water
Coming up against the rocks and trees along the shore.
And the spotted animals in the leaves have begun breathing.
For centuries in China the sky was painted on moonless nights;
What did the civet cats, martens, and black bear of Liaosi Lake
Do watching soldiers with torches touching
Off rockets beside an old pavilion of wet banyan leaves:

The white Calomel Fountain goes up blazing with the low fire
Of three Blue Suns, and you can make out
The terraced hillside with the tallow and yew trees,
Pine and willow, and the orange brick pagoda by a stream
Where two priests are eating melons and roots.

There was an owl in the yew tree: his eyes like twin lakes,
And the two large wooden boats are now being rowed back
To the beach where the children are letting go
Of their mothers' dresses, where watermelons
Are divided by a long, curved blade and night bathers
Are drying in the cold in the light of two fires.
A girl sits on a log

And closes her eyes wanting to see again the blues and yellows,
The falling chains of The Chinese Fire & Rain;
Her older sister is far up the beach past the rocks
And she is nude after swimming with a friend, he drags
A daylily over her stomach and she shuts her eyes.
She, also, sees the ghostly paper chains
Falling out of the black sky into the water. She kisses

Her friend and quickly they run into the trees,
And as with the fireworks, the image
Of their white buttocks stays behind in the mind
Of a young raccoon who's on the rocks trembling,
The dark circles around his eyes are increasingly
Larger like the circles of broken water
On the lake where a fish has just jumped for a deerfly:

This, then, was midsummer, not a new season:

It's Isiah Potter's sermon about the green tips
Of things, a green conclusion to everything.
Accept death, he says, don't fear the daffodils
That pierce your chest or the ones that are burning
As they arc through the open windows of your houses.

Isiah Potter walked solemnly from his old saltbox
And tar-shingle house onto a stone walk
And looked up the street past the roses
To the Orient. (He woke a lunatic.) It was
The Sabbath, and he worked on his sermon
As he walked toward the meetinghouse: the green things,

The judgments, and the faintings in the first garden
In the gilded book, the monotony of an animal or angel,
The couple nude beside the rocks, and

He thought: the eyes of the owl are twin, green lakes
As it glides down from its tree in China, closing, now,
On a field mouse where suddenly there are four rockets

Climbing: a white fountain and three blue suns burning
And the owl crumpled on the terraced hillside. Also,

He thought,
The bald heads of two priests can be seen
Like the white buttocks of the lovers fleeing into the trees.

    III. 1922

The old woman is on her side on the sofa: the vase
Beside her is a fountain of red straw.
The old woman
Has been dead for some time now.

She drank her tea and stretched out on the sofa.
She looked out the open window
Across the street to where under the trees
The local orchestra was beginning something small
By Debussy. She watched a boy
Lift his tuba off the grass.
And with his first clear note she began to chill;
Her eyes never closed. She was just there
In her purple dress on the sofa. And
Through the open window all that night the boy
With the tuba was watched as if by an animal
Or monarch. You know how passengers

On a train prepare themselves
For a tunnel: they are watching the fir trees
That darken the hillsides while, separate and shy,
They begin to enter a mountain, they straighten
Under the white ropes and cool purple curtains:

There's a fat woman
Over there who neglects her lapdog and looks
As if she was stabbed in the neck, the banker
Beside you was maybe kicked by a horse in the head,
And even the child across from you
Stops sucking on her mother's breast and looks up
Having swallowed perhaps a coin or hatpin.

The victims of composition as dead passengers
On a train each secretly positioned
For a dark passage through rock where the ocher deer
Stand frozen, where everyone stops talking

To watch like the old woman on the sofa
Staring past her open window for a week, wanting
Very much to be discovered, she looks almost alive
Like the elephant gone perfectly still
In the mountain pass after hearing a train rush
By below him; he sniffs the air
And glances down into a forest where like him
Everything alive has stopped moving for the moment.
The train went by. The local orchestra sits
In its folding chairs and sips away at sherry,
All of them that is
But the boy with a tuba who looks
Across the street to an open window and farther even

Into the dark house
Where nothing has moved for hours, where
You'll hear a voice that's not enough,
That speaks to us under the trees
Just before the white baton flies up:

What it says might be read aloud to children:
Tell me about the woman of many turns
Who had her tables cleaned with sponges
Who walked the beach like a motionless

Moving elephant
And who talked to the hyacinth, gull, and ant.
Tell me about the woman of many turns.

And tell me you can't...

Only if it had been a rainy morning
There wouldn't have been
The freshly cut flowers in the hall,
Or in the garden in the sun
The small toad wouldn't have thought her straw hat
Was a second sun that had cooled
Like everything else around her.

Only if it had rained along the coast
All that morning outside her open window.
If she wasn't in the garden in the morning
She would have been alive to see
The silver tuba like a snail
Returned to the grass after the concert.

The butterfly buttons its shirt twice
In the afternoon. After working
All morning in the garden she walked
Down to the ocean and looked across to France

Where the ocher deer have stood motionless
On the cave walls for centuries.
To the hyacinth she speaks French. She doesn't
Speak to us at all. This collector of black tea:
Souchong and orange pekoe brewed with the seeds
Of the St. Ignatius' bean, swallowed hurriedly
In the shade of a little country parlor. *She doesn't*

Speak to us at all.

Does the barbarian cutting the throat
Of a speckled doe in China ever enjoy his solitude?
Perhaps, he's always been alone
Like the corpse dressed in purple on the sofa.
They were both strong.
They have both eaten venison.
Their venison is historical and ocher.

How do we remember them? Let me
Tell you about this woman
Who's resting on the sofa
Like a fawn fading into leaves and rocks.
She's positioned for entering

A tunnel, and, yet, for her it was simply
An open window through which a boy
Reaches out for his tuba smiling

Like the Hun
Who's charging through the Empress Dowager's
Gardens, leaning down
From his horse he grabs a virgin by the hair
And lifts her off the grass

And having seen enough, this ordinary old woman
Saw an end to her suffering. *And, then,*

A white baton flew up!

Ghost

If a man stands by a pin oak emptying
A thermos onto the ground and it is cold
In the light, and the light itself
Has condensed
Inside his bones, would you walk up to him
And say, "I went to the clay house. It still
Smells of the hickory, even now in November.
I want to know what is going
To happen to everyone"?
The sound of churchbells comes out of
The canebrake.
The insides of three birds are smoking
On the ground by his feet. He watches

A leaf come all the way down out
Of its tree. Then he speaks, "Look, little pigeon,
What are you doing
Out here in your nightgown? Your hair
Is wet. You're standing in your bare feet
Like the girls down in the cabins.
You should have visited me earlier: I waited
For you here each evening in the summer. I covered
The bird entrails with leaves.
There was a smell of plums. The fox
Was in the clearing. Does your mother
Forgive me. I didn't mean to... you tell

Me 'that's loss' and 'that's dead'
And 'I don't remember ever owning a red dress.'
You know that night before I went into
The fields, as much as she had hurt me in the afternoon,
I laid down the gun

To draw water in the tub for her. She should
Find that a pleasant memory.

Tell her they were wrong. 'It could have been
An accident.'
When I went out the door the tub
Was still filling and she called to me
That she'd see to it. I have a memory of her, naked
Running to a tub as if to someone, and
Her mouth is opening. She kneels almost
Without getting near it, and, out of breath,
Just stares at the faucets for a moment; then reaches
Touching the collar of the coat. I am bleeding.
Leaves are stuck to my chest. Then, there's
A sound she hears down in the cane, and
Really it's much more
Than a sound, but not yet a noise.

It's like a tub overflowing onto a floor."

The City of the Olesha Fruit

for Barry Goldensohn

The spider vanished at the boy's mere
Desire to touch it with his hand.
YURI OLESHA

Outside the window past the two hills there is the city
Where the color-blind are waking to blue pears;
Also, there are the blue treetops waving
To the schoolgirls who step harshly along
In winter dresses: out of the mouths of these girls
Come the cones, their breath,
A mist like the silver ear trumpets
Of deaf children tipped toward whatever it is
They are almost hearing.

An old man without legs, not yet in a chair, has
Invented the city outside the window.
And everywhere now it is morning! He hears

His wife climbing the stairs.
What, he thinks… what to do?
The strong line of her back
Is like a spoon.
He says, "Good morning and how are you?"
She says, "Rumen,
I told you the hen should have been put
Up with straw in the attic. Last night the fox
Ate all of her but the dark spurs under the chin
And a few feathers."

His wife gathers him up in her arms, walks to the far
Corner of the room, and lowers him into a straight chair

Beside a table. Only last year he would sit
And stare at the shoes he could wear, without socks

And with the laces loose.
A tub is filling in another room.

He thinks, "Poor Widow is inside the stomach
Of a fox. My wife's idea was not a good one:
Where would Widow have found the scratch
And gravel for her shells while up in the attic?
And what about
The rooster! What about the poor rooster
On his railing by the barn; inconsolable, crowing?"
Rumen remembers a Russian story about a copper rooster
With a green fern for a tail.
Rumen's favorite writer is the great Russian
Yuri Olesha. Rumen thinks, "Yes, Yuri, my companion,
There is cruelty in the format of a kiss!
And the blue skins of pears
In a heap on a dish leave a memory

Of myself as a boy running along the flume water
Down past the village ditch.
But, Yuri, in my city all the streets are,
Just this moment, being swept: old women
In jade dresses sweeping, sweeping.
And soon it will rain for them and then
I'll return their sun, a noon sun
To take away the wet before the children
Rush out under the bells for an hour's recess.

Oh, Yuri, just beyond the grin of a smelly
Old fox, that's where Widow is, our best hen!
Yuri, my legs, I think, are buried in the orchard
Beside the stable where the hospital horses
Of my city wait, poised for an emergency.
These horses are constant; how they race

Down the cobbled streets for me. They've never
Trampled the children!"

"Rumen," his wife called, "do you want a haircut
This morning?" She steps into the room.

He smiles at her. She is buttoning her blouse.
And she smiles back to him. Rumen would say

To Yuri that sometimes her yellow hair
Got into the corners of his mouth.
"And, Yuri, that was when I most missed my youth."
Then Rumen would again fall silent.
He was off opening a raincloud over his city.
It was winter when he woke, but now I'm sure it's
Not. There are a few dark flowers?
Rumen feels that it is best for the children
If they walk to school in the clear winter air, but
Once he gets around to raining on his trees,
Streets, and houses, well, then he changes everything
To late July or August.
But the evenings in his city are always
Placed in autumn: there is the smell
Of woodsmoke, so pleasant,
And leaves burning. Flocks of bluebirds would be
Flying south.

And so there is the obscurity of many lives,
Not yours, Olesha, but mine and my wife's,
Two characters
Who are, perhaps, in a shade
Just now sipping an iced summer tea
With its twigs and leaves floating around inside:

We are giggling, I think, about how shy
We were as lovers that first winter night
When I kissed her in the dark barn

Right in her open eye. I tried again
And missed again. To accidentally kiss a young girl

In her open eye is, I think,
The beginning of experience. *Yuri,*
I did find her mouth that night!

But then the following winter, a week before
Our wedding, I missed again, this time
I kissed a small bare breast.
That wasn't an accident—

She reached out to touch my hand
And found my thigh!
The shyness of lovers, as softly, at night,
They miss and miss while following an old map, yes,
The format of a kiss.
In the city of the Olesha fruit

A citizen never dies, he just wakes
One morning without his legs, and then he is given
A city of his very own making:

In this way his existence narrows
While expanding like a diary, or
Like this landscape with two hills
Seen through my window early
Each and every winter morning! But, Yuri,
Outside this window—yes, I know,

What's there is there, and all of it
Indelible as our memory of blue pears, washed
And being eaten in the sunlight of a city
That is being constructed all of the time,
Its new gold domes and towers,
Just beyond two hills in the winter air, and
Somewhere inside the mind.

The Seagull

Chekhov, at Yalta

A winter evening at the cottage by the bay,
And I sat in the black and gold of the dead garden
Wrapped in blankets, eating my sister's suet pudding.
The fountain was wrapped in dirty straw and

Just below my property in the old Tartar cemetery
There was a small funeral in progress: the widow
Is wearing a purple shawl, the children are bare around
The shoulders and the girls are wearing orange petals

At their throats. The ashen white beards of the men
Are like immaculate vests from this distance.
There is nothing more intolerable than suet pudding,
Unless it is the visitors. The drunken visitors laughing

In my kitchen, eating my duck and venison, while I hide
From them here in the dark garden.
The daughter of one of these gentlemen is pretty.
I saw her through the window drinking

Champagne from a clay mug—just under her thin blouse
I saw the blue points of her breasts that turn,
In opposition, both out and up like the azure slippers
Of the priest who is now singing in the cemetery below my house.

Once the family has gone off with its torches I'll
Climb down to the fresh grave and drop some coins
For flowers, even wooden teeth for the widow so she can

Attract a new husband? The black, turned soil
Of our garden reminds me

Of the common grave given to the children
Of the Godunov Orphanage after that horrible fire:

A charred horse was thrown in with them,
Bags of lime, and what I understood to be a large ham
That the authorities, nevertheless, declared
The torso of a male child of nine or ten. The Czar,

In their memory, placed a tiny trout pond over them
And this inscription: *A blue blanket for my little ones.*
My wife goes nearly naked to parties in Moscow.
My sister here, at Yalta, goes sea bathing with a rope

Around her that runs back to the beach where it is
Attached to a donkey who is commanded by a servant
With a long switch.
The sea tows her out and then the donkey is whipped

Sorrowfully until he has dragged her back to them.
I named the donkey, Moon, after the mystery of his service
To my sister. This winter
He has been an excellent friend.

I read to this poor beast from *Three Sisters.* He is a better
Critic and audience than I could find in the cities.
I have won an Award that will save me from arrest anywhere
Inside Russia. I am going to refuse it! And then travel

To Nice or Paris.
My tuberculosis is worse. Tolstoi reads my stories
To his family after supper. And reads them badly, I suppose!
I did walk that evening all the way down to the cemetery

Only to discover that my pockets were empty.
I screamed up to the house for coins, for plenty
Of coins! The visitors, laughing and singing, ran down
To me without coats and with a lantern swinging—

My sister trailed behind them
On her donkey. Her square black hat
Bobbing like a steamer way out in the bay.
And when they reached me —

I said, "Sister, pack the trunks! You hurt me!
I will write that we have departed for France, for Italy."

A Widow Speaks to the Auroras of a December Night

My yard with its pines is almost spherical in winter.

The green awning outside the window is torn
By heavy snow. I sit in the cane chair.
Beside me, within reach, the gramophone grinds out
A little Debussy: the horn
Of the gramophone is plugged with a sock.

An artery stands out at my ankle
And these little crossings
Of blood do blossom secretly in the leg, climbing
Up to the heart or lungs. There's the
Familiar light coming on in the distance in the dark city:

It has been a spark within a house above my pines
Before sunrise each winter for these
Past three years of just tea and the *Times.*
I often remember
An especially dry gin from the barroom
At the Ritz Tower. The watercolor my husband purchased
In Caracas remains in the corner
Bound in twine and dark caramel papers; it has a
Big postage stamp depicting a native girl
Holding up a blue turtle.

The familiar light above the pines goes out. A man
Has dipped both of his hands into a stream of cold water.
He has washed his teeth and hair. Clean-shaven,
He greets his wife in their kitchen. She has fried
Some trout with bacon. Outside my window the sapphire light
Of the northeast-Packet plane lifts up out of Hartford,

Its soft, watery light dips and then
Leans into a sunrise:
There is snow, pines, and two sheep who have wandered
From a neighbor's farm beyond the reservoir—
Just this winter scene, and two wide sheep that
Are the blue-white of a chunk of fat

Falling off the dangerous, true edge of daylight.

The Hours

for Ingrid Erhardt, 1951–1971

The meadows are empty. There are two villages:
One to the north and another to the south.
It's first light, and the two villages are striking
Their two bells. This is a green valley
That has an echo. Now, the bell to the south
Follows immediately the bell in the north.
So when the bell to the north is struck
Its echo is not heard by anyone for it is lost
In the sound from the south. A pilgrim
Has just climbed down into the valley.
Does he believe that he hears
One, two, or four bells working in the morning?

This much is clear: when the bells stopped
The pilgrim thought, at first, that he had
Heard last that bell to the north, followed
By the bell to the south, followed by the echo
Of the bell to the south. So he would tell us
That there are three bells being struck
In the morning. But
You know how after hearing bells
You seem to carry them around
For some time inside your skull? And, also,
The echo of the bell to the north that is lost
So often each morning, where does it go?

Perhaps, it goes where the pilgrim is going. And
Neither north, nor south. We will all be lost,
Even down to the very last memories that others have
Of us, and then these others who survived us, they

Too will be lost. There were many more bells
Than we thought, they will

Never stop for us, as waking to them we realize that
Throughout our lives, in the light and in the dark,

We were always counting our losses.

After Three Photographs of Brassaï

A whore moves a basin of green antiseptic water
Away from the towels to a clean white shelf.
A Russian sailor rests against the wall smelling
Of tobacco.

The tall narrow mirror has little dark flecks
Within it like the black sinks of a smoky surgical theater
Seen from the balconies: the whore
From *above* is now below us, in the future, on a table where

Two students in white gowns are struggling to open her:
The ribs cracking back, the pink gill-like trench
Follows the thin hairline down the center
Of her stomach to where the knife shallows on pelvic bone.

A student beside us vomits and his breakfast of warm milk
Falls slowly to the floor passing tier after tier
Of first-year students. The autopsy is over.
The charwoman in a yellow bonnet is mopping up.

Now the same dead girl is, again, moving the green water
Away from the soiled towels. A banker
Smelling of jasmine is dressing himself. The whore straightens
Her shoulders, this girl who is always bent

Over herself. Her fingers which she chews are hurt
By an acid douche. She straightens her shoulders
As she stares into a black speck in the mirror so as
To forget. She begins singing, also, to forget;

The banker stepping into his taxi is trying to remember
If there was a mole on her neck, if this one's name
Was Claudette? And he is stepping into the taxi, he is
Drunk and falling into the blackness of it: his shoe flies

Up into the night as high as the colored numerals and lights.
The door slams shut. The charwoman has finished mopping up,
She turns out the lights. You are now alone in the upper-
Most balcony looking down for a floor through the darkness.

You drop a pencil waiting to hear it strike the boards...
It falls stiff like a drunk, like a drunk falling onto a whore.

The Dun Cow and the Hag

Beside the river Volga near the village of Anskijovka
On a bright summer day

An old woman sat sewing
By the riverbank. If asked she would say

She was lowering the hem of a black dress.
All the while she sewed

A cow stood beside her. They were ignored
As the day passed; by evening, a merchant

From Novgorod arrived with his family
At the riverbank carrying baskets.

His eldest daughter down beyond a clump
Of white birches undressed and stepped

Into the river, the girl's breasts
Are large and moved separately like twins

Handed from one serf to the next
Down to a river for baptism. The merchant,

His wife, and their son are seated
In the grass eating chunks of pink fish

That they dip in scented butter. The fish
Spoiled as it rode in the sun on the top

Of their carriage. These three have been poisoned
And can be seen kneeling in the grass.

The daughter who was bathing in the river
Is, now, crying for anyone to help her: the hag

Leaves her cow to walk down to the floundering girl:
Just her arms above the water

Working like scissors.
She cut the thread for the old woman.

It was summertime on the river Volga, and the old woman
Told the cow

That this could happen to anyone and that
It *had* happened once to them; and

It was summertime on the river Volga,
The black water

Ran off her dress like a lowered hem.

Elegy to the Sioux

The vase was made of clay
With spines of straw
For strength. The sunbaked vase
Soaked in a deep blue dye for days. The events in this wilderness,
Portrayed in the round of the vase,

Depend on shades of indigo against
The masked areas of the clay, a flat pearl color
To detail the big sky and snow...

This Montana field in winter is not sorrowful:
A bugle skips through notes:

We view it all somehow from the center of the field
And there are scattered groups of cavalry. Some of these
Men were seasoned by civil war. Their caps are blue.
Their canteens are frozen. The horses shake their heads
Bothered by the beads of ice, the needles of ice
Forming at both sides of their great anvil heads.

The long, blue cloaks of the officers fall over the haunches
Of the horses. The ammunition wagons
Beside the woods are blurred by the snowy weather...

Beyond the wagons, farther even, into the woods
There is a sloping streambed. This is
The dark side of the vase which is often misunderstood.
From here through the bare trees there's
A strange sight to be seen at the very middle of the field:

A valet is holding a bowl of cherries — archetype and rubric,
A general with white hair eats the fruit while introducing its color
Which will flow through the woods in early December.

An Indian woman came under dark clouds to give birth, unattended
In the deep wash inside the woods. She knew the weather

Could turn and staked the tips of two rooted spruce trees
To the earth to make a roof.
The deerskin of her robe is in her mouth. Her legs spread,
Her feet are tied up in the roof of darkening spruce. *No stars
Show through!* But on the vase that belonged to a President
There are countless stars above the soldiers' campfires...

With rawhide her feet are tied high in the spruce
And her right hand is left loose as if she were about
To ride a wild stallion
                                to its conclusion in a box canyon.

President Grant drinks bourbon from his boot. The Sioux
Cough in their blankets...

It snowed an hour more, and then the moon appeared. The
                        unborn infant,
Almost out on the forest floor, buckled and lodged. It died.
Its mother died. Just before she closed her eyes
She rubbed snow up and down the inside of her bare thighs.

In the near field an idle, stylish horse raised one leg
To make a perfect right angle. Just then a ghost of snow formed
Over the tents of the soldiers,

It blows past the stylish, gray horse,
Unstopped it moves through woods, up the streambed,
And passes into the crude spruce shelter, into the raw open
Woman, her legs raised into sky—
Naked house of snow and ice! This gust of wind

Spent the night within the woman. At sunrise, it left her mouth
Tearing out trees, keeping the owls from sleep; it was angry now

And into the field it spilled, into the bivouac of pony soldiers
Who turned to the south, who turned back to the woods, who became

Still. Blue all over! If there is snow still unspooling in the mountains
Then there is time yet for the President to get his Indian vase
And to fill it with bourbon from his boot and to put flowers into it:
The flowers die in a window that looks out on a cherry tree
Which heavy with fruit drops a branch:

                                        torn to its very heartwood
By the red clusters of fruit, the branch fell
Like her leg and foot
Out of the sky into Montana...

A Grandfather's Last Letter

Elise, I have your valentine with the red shoes. I have
Waited too many weeks to write—wanting to describe
The excitement on the back lawn for you:
                                        the forsythia

Is now a bright yellow, and with the ribbons you draped
Inside it, trembles in a breeze,
All yellow and blues, like that pilot light this winter
Worried by just a little breath that came out of you.

On the dark side of the barn there's the usual railing
Of snow.
The tawny owl, nightingales, and moles
Have returned to the lawn again.

I have closed your grandmother's front rooms.

I know you miss her too. Her crocus bed showed its first
Green nose this morning. For breakfast I had
A duck's egg and muffins.

Your father thinks I shouldn't be alone?
Tell him I have planted a row of volunteer radishes.
I have replaced the north window...

So you have read your first book. Sewed a dress for
The doll. The very young and old are best at finding
Little things to do. The world is jealous of us, you know?

The moles are busy too. Much more mature this year,
The boar with the black velvet coat made a twelve-
Foot-long gallery under the linden where the mockingbirds
Are nesting.

The moles took some of my rags to add to
Their nursery of grass, leaves, and roots.
The cream-colored sow is yet to make her appearance!
They have seven mounds. Each with three bolt doors
Or holes. The pine martens are down from the woods, I see them
In the moonlight waiting for a kill.

Molehills can weaken a field so that a train
Passing through it sinks suddenly, the sleepers
In their berths sinking too!

I wonder what it's like in their underground rooms:
Their whiskers telegraphing the movements
Of earthworms. They don't require water when on
A steady diet of night crawlers. Worms are almost
Entirely made of water.

Last night there was quite an incident. The sun was going
Down and the silly boar was tunneling toward
The linden and he went shallow, the owl dropped down
Setting its claws into the lawn, actually taking hold
Of the blind mole, at that moment the mockingbird,
Thinking her nest threatened, fell on the owl putting
Her tiny talons into his shoulders. Well,

There they were, Elise, the owl on top of the invisible
Mole, the mockingbird on top of the owl. The mole
Moved backward a foot,
The birds were helpless and moved with him.
They formed quite a totem. The two birds looked so serious
In their predicament. A wind brushed the wash on the line.
And our three friends broke each for its respective zone.

Tomorrow the vines on the house are coming down. I want
The warmth of the sun on that wall. I'm sending
You a package with some of your grandmother's old clay
Dolls, silverware, and doilies.

Tell your father he is not coming in June to kill
The moles! Tell him to go fishing instead, or to take
Your mother to Florida.

You said you worry that someday I'll be dead also! Well,
Elise, of course, I will. I'll be hiding then from your world
Like our moles. They move through their tunnels
With a swimming motion. They don't know where they're going —

But they go.

There's more to this life than we know. If ever
You're sleeping in a train on the northern prairies
And everything sinks a little
But keeps on going, then, you've visited me in another world —

Where I am going.

The Ganges

for Kaya

I'm sorry but we can't go to the immersions tonight
For the poor will not get down from the wheel, and
The musicians and the lorry won't budge
Without the money. We don't have it. But, we could

Walk to the cremations. It will be dark with a mist
Where the stairs jump into the water. These are
The funeral ghats. The corpses are brought in drapes
And that one will be dipped in the river and then
She will be anointed with clarified butter. To the
Left of us four men waist-deep in the river sift
Through mud and ashes for gold rings.
With a straw torch
The dead mother's son starts the fire;
With a bone cudgel
He smashes her skull to release the images shared
By her with these

Postcards I am now passing to you:
Of the family pond entirely filled with limes,
White pigs rooting in coconut husks, and her six
Children watering their charges, the black lulled elephants.

Elegy to the Pulley of Superior Oblique

for Lipita, Tito, and Joaquin

The three girls in a donkey cart are
Ascending the tiled adobe bridge, its little arc
Over the dry wash under a noonday sun. Below them
A wizened farmer with a bag of grain sleeps in the shadows
Of the bridge while sitting on the dry river
Bottom which looks like a long black skid mark
Vanishing off the side of a cliff on the highway beyond
The purple mountains.

There are miserable people, standing for the duration
In a halated light, whom I would never describe

For it would be a lie. To write, for example, that
Two houseflies are like two fiddles drying
In a mahogany vise beside
The blue chisels and almond pastes; that all over the shop
Fans are blowing across huge blocks of ice—
That would be a lie! There's blood on an apron and
The green checkered bills in the cigar box. And
The carpenter's wife is a Jew. This is Warsaw ten years
Before my birth. The sweltering ghetto! Months later,
The sweltering snow!

So I must tell you that the sisters in the cart are
Unhappy and not beautiful. They have suffered scabs and
Diarrhea. They have boiled water out in their yard,
Beside the deep, fragrant cilia plants, and had been too weak
To drag the scalded water a foot or two beyond the fire.
They have all fainted, once or twice,
While squatting in the trench out behind their barn.
This influenza killed their mother. And aunt.

And, now, they have crossed the bridge and the donkey
Looks under his belly, slumps to one side, and falls
Dead.
The youngest sister begins to sob.
The oldest jumps from the cart and runs down a pebble slope
To the sleeping farmer.
The farmer wakes, frightened, not for a moment looking
Away from the girl's chest that is running with sores.
He says, "A man is taking our picture from above!"
The toothless farmer then waves to Weston, and
The girl slumps onto the brown riverbed with her arms
Around herself.
There are dogs sniffing near the donkey.
There are two flies. And

What does this girl have to do with
Our lives? That excellent man, *Rosen,* knows:

Open your eyes: there's sky, mountains; the moment
Of death is instant, contrived.

Thomas Hardy

The first morning after anyone's death, is it important
To know that fields are wet, that the governess is
Naked but with a scarf still covering her head, that
She's sitting on a gardener who's wearing
Just a blue shirt, or that he's sitting on a chair in the kitchen.
They look like they are rowing while instead outside in the mist
Two boats are passing on the river, the gardener's mouth
Is opening:

A white, screaming bird lifts off the river into the trees,
Flies a short distance and is joined
By a second bird, but then as if to destroy everything
The two white birds are met by a third. *The night
Always fails.* The cows are now standing in the barns.
You can hear the milk as it drills into wooden pails.

Grand Illusion

*My father had several times expressed a fear of being
buried alive. I insisted that the doctor should do what-
ever was necessary. The doctor asked me to leave the
room. When I came back, he was able to assure me that
Renoir was dead!*

JEAN RENOIR

It is not 1937 for long. A clump of ash trees and a walk
Down to the boathouse: inside linen is tacked up
In a long blank mural; the children sit on the wings
Of the dry dock, and then, over the water in a circle
Of rowboats, the aunts and uncles wait while
At their center the projectionist, Jean Renoir,
On a cedar raft, casts silhouettes of rabbits, birds,
And turtles for the sleepy children. Corks
Come out of old bottles, it is a few minutes past sunset
And, now, a swimmer beside the raft looks

Into the boathouse to the linens: *at last, it is 1915!*
A bird screams over the lake, two bats
Flitter back and forth through the beam of the lamp,
Interrupting the images, the grand illusion, cast over
Water to the acceptance of white tablecloths
On the darkening shore of the lake. A torch is lit
For its kerosene smoke is repugnant to the swarming insects.
This film and its prisoners exist between extreme borders,
Not music and algebra but
A war and, then, yet another war...

But we begin with the captured officers digging
A tunnel that will soon be outside the garden wall.
The Boches observe the Frenchmen working
With their hoes as from the trousers of a boy
Dirt from the tunnel secretly spills onto horse manure!

The prisoners dream of crossing a meadow filled
With snow, in the moonlight it is jade-green snow
While Germans with rifles on a hill
Are unable to kill them, for they have escaped
Into Switzerland with its feather-brushed trees

And patina of copper rooftops along a hillside village.
Isn't this the ending of the film?
No! I'm sorry but
There is a single blossom
On the geranium, and when it falls, Captain de Boeldieu
Dies, discovering his afterlife along a November road—
He does not know that two men are hiding in the marsh
Beside him; nevertheless, it is at this moment that the film
Suffers its true conclusion. The two men hiding
In the marsh will escape across the border, only
To be returned to the continuing war. This is why there
Is no importance to your version of the story. And there
Will be another war. And more horror for the geranium!
So, to pass the time, the imprisoned soldiers receive
A steamer trunk filled with women's clothing.
They will all perform in a revue: a chorus
Of boys and men, rouge and talcum, black stockings,
Garters, the *tonneau* dresses, false breasts and
Large paper carnations riding up like epaulets

On their broad shoulders. These poignant inversions
Are not ridiculous: the third boy from the right
Has delicate milky thighs, these women are not ridiculous
Until they begin to stiffen into men as they sing,
In this comedy, their national anthem! The Russian
Prisoners have been given a trunk, also, from their
Mysterious Czarina; the men open it expecting vodka
And sausages. The box is filled with straw
And books on cooking, painting, and algebra. In disgust
They burn these books—kiss good-bye the frontier

Of algebra and the desire for wedding tripe!
Now, these officers who are escape artists are moved
As an elite corps and north to Wintersborn. Later,
They are taken to a damp limestone castle
From which no one will escape. The Commandant
Is the stoic aristocrat, Rauffenstein, his head is in
A brace like a white egg in a silver teaspoon.
I mean no disrespect, but the balding Rauffenstein is
An abject picture of suffering. His villa has but one
Flower, a tall laden geranium.

Rauffenstein and the other aristocrat, Boeldieu,
Are friends. Both would know that to clear a monocle
One uses spirits of vinegar. They stand confirmed
In manner beside a squirrel cage. Rauffenstein feels
Superior to the other two principals, the rich
Jew, Rosenthal, and the charming emotional Marechal.
These two hide in the marsh while Boeldieu dies
Of a bullet wound. Only a king may kill a king!
And Rauffenstein did it with his pistol; taking aim
But missing the leg; he severed in three places
Boeldieu's intestine!

The Captain is given a room in the turret that holds
The flowering geranium. Now comes the *oratio obliqua*
Of the marksman, Rauffenstein; the disfigured Commandant
Is sincerely saddened
At having killed the noble Captain. But before
The shooting and escape we sensed the Captain's
Sacrifice was not sacrifice, or suicide, but
The grand escape — a country road into another landscape…
There are bells tolling down in the village.
Rosenthal and Marechal with ropes have dropped

Past the castle's battlements to the ground.
They run away across snowy farmland. Marechal's teeth
Are stained from chewing licorice-flavored tobacco.

Rosenthal and Marechal are extremes who have
Strong feelings for each other. They are befriended
By a German widow, Ulsa, and her daughter, Lotte;
Ulsa sleeps with the tall handsome Jew. He promises
To return for her when the war is over. He
Will lose both his legs at Mégéglise.
This is not known within the story, but he'll bleed

To death beside a little bridge. He lived his illusion
In the Orient of Delacroix, his servants were Syrians
And Negroes. He loved the little ivory spoons that
Chinese women in the open markets use to bathe
And freshen the exotic tiny fish they sell out
Of huge clay bowls…
In the boathouse the children sleep, while Jean's
Oldest cousin, drunken, falls out of a rowboat.
The lone swimmer has joined Renoir on the raft.
The film now reveals the *first diversion*
As all of the prisoners of the fortress begin playing
Several hundred wooden flutes, the noise is like women
Crying over the fresh mounds at Verdun. This diversion
Is not illusion
And as the Boches collect the flutes, the drunken cousin
Tries to join Renoir on the raft. Boeldieu flees
To the heights of the castle, the second diversion!
We hear: *Halt! Halt! Halt!*
A gunshot, and chowder with blood falls from Boeldieu's
Opened stomach all the way down to the courtyard.

There are small fish bones in the viscera on the cobbled
Courtyard floor. Scissors cut the blue blossom
From the geranium. Boeldieu will die… dead,
He awakens on a country road where, now a peasant,
He walks a white horse under the looming, bare trees.
Rosenthal and Marechal are watching
As they hide in the dead marsh flowers of
An early November. They are alive. They do not

Recognize their friend. Renoir's cousin, asking for
More wine, climbing onto the raft, spills

Everything, and the projector with its crude lamp
Sinks slowly to the bottom of the lake —
Its dusky lighted windows like a bathysphere
Lost off a cable that frayed, whoever is alive
Inside the iron bell is experiencing
An eternal falling through water without the promise
Of a bottom... it's 1937, the children
Asleep in the boathouse are being aroused, they wake
To a bat caught in the wall of linen, they think it's
Their uncle still casting images of animals for them...

You

for Jody

The sunlight passes through the window into the room
Where you are sewing a button to your blouse: outside
Water in the fountain rises
Toward a cloud. This plume of water is lighter
Now, for white shares of itself are falling back
Toward the ground.
This water does succeed, like us,
In nearing a perfect exhaustion,
Which is its origin. The water

Succeeds in leaving the ground but
It fails at its desire to reach a cloud. It pauses,
Falling back into its blue trough; of course,
Another climb is inevitable, and this loud, falling
Water is a figure for love, not loss, and

Still heavy with its desire to be the cloud.

Elizabeth's War with the Christmas Bear

The bears are kept by hundreds within fences, are fed cracked
Eggs; the weakest are
Slaughtered and fed to the others after being scented
With the blood of deer brought to the pastures by Elizabeth's
Men — the blood spills from deep pails with bottoms of slate.

The balding Queen had bear gardens in London and in the country.
The bear is baited: the nostrils
Are blown full with pepper, the Irish wolf dogs
Are starved, then, emptied, made crazy with fermented barley:

And the bear's hind leg is chained to a stake, the bear
Is blinded and whipped, kneeling in his own blood and slaver, he is
Almost instantly worried by the dogs. At the very moment that
Elizabeth took Essex's head, a giant brown bear
Stood in the gardens with dogs hanging from his fur...
He took away the sun, took
A wolfhound in his mouth, and tossed it into
The white lap of Elizabeth 1 — arrows and staves rained

On his chest, and standing, he, then, stood even taller, seeing
Into the Queen's private boxes — he grinned
Into her battered eggshell face.
Another volley of arrows and poles, and opening his mouth
He showered
Blood all over Elizabeth and her Privy Council.

The very next evening, a cool evening, the Queen demanded
Thirteen bears and the justice of 113 dogs: she slept

All that Sunday night and much of the next morning.
Some said she was guilty of *this* and *that*.
The Protestant Queen gave the defeated bear

A grave in a Catholic cemetery. The marker said:
Peter, a Solstice Bear, a gift of the Tsarevitch to Elizabeth.

After a long winter she had the grave opened. The bear's skeleton
Was cleared with lye, she placed it at her bedside,
Put a candle inside behind the sockets of the eyes, and, then
She spoke to it:

You were a Christmas bear—behind your eyes
I see the walls of a snow cave where you are a cub still smelling
Of your mother's blood which has dried in your hair; you have
Troubled a Queen who was afraid
When seated in *shade* which, standing,
You had created! A Queen who often wakes with a dream
Of you at night—
Now, you'll stand by my bed in your long white bones; alone, you
Will frighten away at night all visions of bear, and all day
You will be in this cold room—your constant grin,
You'll stand in the long, white prodigy of your bones, and you are,

Every inch of you, a terrible vision, not bear, but virgin!

Aubade of the Singer and Saboteur, Marie Triste

In the twenties, I would visit Dachau often with my brother.
There was then an artists' colony outside the Ingolstadt Woods
And these estates had a meadow filled
With the hazy blood-campion, sumac, and delicate yellow cinquefoil.
At the left of the meadow there was a fast stream and pond, and
Along the stream, six lodges and the oak Dachau Hall where
Meals were held and the evening concerts. In winter, the Hall
Was a hostel for hunters, and the violinists, who were the first
Of the colony to arrive in spring, would spend three days
Scouring the deer blood off the floors, tables, walls, and sinks.
They would rub myrtle leaves into the wood to get out the stink!

The railway from Munich to Ingolstadt would deposit us by
The gold water tower, and my brother, Charles, and I would cut
Across two fields to the pastures behind Dachau Hall. Once,
Crossing these fields, Charles, who had been drinking warm beer
Since morning, stopped, and crouching low in the white chicory
And lupine found a single, reddish touch-me-not which is rare
Here in the mountains. A young surgeon, Charles assumed his
Condescending tone, and began by saying, "Now, sister,

This flower has no perfume — what you smell is not your
Brother's breath either, but the yeast sheds of the brewery just over
That hill. This uncommon flower can grow to an enormous height
If planted in water. It is a succulent annual. Its private
Appointments are oval and its nodding blossom takes its weight
From pods with crimson threadlike supports." With his bony fingers

He began to force open the flower. I *blushed.* He said, "It is
A devoted, sexual flower; its tough, meatlike labia protrude
Until autumn and then shrivel; this adult flower

If disturbed explodes *into a small yellow rain like*
That fawn we watched urinating on the hawthorn just last August."

Charles was only two years older but could be a wicked fellow.
Once, on our first day at the colony, at midnight, he was
Discovered nude and bathing in the pond with a cellist. She was
The only cellist, and for that week, Charles was their only doctor.
So neither was banished. But neither was spoken to except
For rehearsals and in illness. There is a short bridge passage
In a Scriabin sonata that reminds me of the bursting touch-me-nots,
That reminds me, also, of Heisdt-Bridge *itself,* in Poland! We blew
It up in October. I had primed the packages of glycerin, kieselguhr,
Woodmeal, and chalk. We curbed the explosives with sulfur.
I sat in primrose and sorrel with the plunger-box and at four o'clock
Up went the munitions shipment from Munich to Warsaw. Those thin
Crimson supports of the flower tossed up like the sunburned arms
Of the pianist Mark Meichnik, arriving at his favorite E-flat-
Major chord; and I guess that whenever a train or warehouse went
Four-ways-to-market right before my eyes, I thought
Of that large moment of Schumann's. The morning
After Heidst-Bridge I was captured and Charles

Was shot.

I was at Dachau by the weekend. They have kept me in
A small cell. A young lieutenant tortured me that first night.
Knowing I was a singer they asked me to perform
For the commandant early the next week.
By then I was able to stand again, but my Nazi inquisitor
Had for an hour touched live wires to me while holding
Me in a shallow ice bath. I had been
Made into a tenor voice! The commandant's wife dismissed me
After a few notes. As I was tortured I forced myself
To dwell on the adult life of the touch-me-not, that fawn in
Hawthorn, and my brother's drunken anatomy lesson that showed
No skill at all there in the silver meadow. I was probably

Stupid not to have fallen unconscious. When I was
Ordered out of the parlor by the Nazi bitch, I did, for the first

Time in two years, cry aloud. I think it was for my voice that
I cried so badly. The guards laughed, returning me to my cell.
My cell has a bench, a pail, and a wire brush. Every two days
Without warning the hose comes alive with water, moving through
The space like a snake. Sometimes it wakes me about the face and legs.
I have lost so much weight that I can sleep comfortably
On the pine bench. I watch shadows in the cell become,
At night, the masquerade dance in the woodcut by Hans Burgkmair:

Its bird shapes, that procession of *men* threading the dance,
And *Maximilian I* greeting them as they twist past the banquet tables.
My inquisitor, all night in the chamber, commanding me
To sing, to sing!

When they fire the ovens out beside the pastures it is like
A giant catching his breath. And then there is the silence
Of the trucks with their murmuring engines. My delusions:
A sound like my brother's cellist, at this early hour, opening
The morning with difficult arm exercises; he said that she would
Play for him naked and until he became jealous. Then I would
Say, "Oh, Charles!" He'd laugh.

My favorite pastime has become the imaginary destruction of flowers.
I hear their screams. They bleed onto the floor of my cell. I scrub
The wall where a *Bürgermeister* opened the artery of a doe that
He had shot just outside the window.
Later, the *Bürgermeister*'s favorite butcher making venison flanks
Into roasts, how he sawed at the large femur of the deer
Like the cellist waking with her instrument, their right arms
Are beautiful with white muscles;
The butcher and the cellist died, here, admiring the noxious
Blue crystals on the floors of the gas chamber: the way,
At first, they darken to indigo and like smoke
Climb over your ankles, reaching your waist—

You fall naked as into the field that is with a breeze turning
All its wildflowers, bladder-campion and myrtle, into
A melody of just three staves written for four voices:

Slaughter and music.
Two of the old miracles. They were not my choices.

The Fox Who Watched for the Midnight Sun

Across the snowy pastures of the estate
Open snares drift like paw prints under rain, everywhere
There is the conjured hare being dragged
Up into blowing snow: it struggles
Upside down by a leg, its belly
Is the slaked white of cottages along the North Sea.

Inside the parlor Ibsen writes of a summer garden, of a
Butterfly sunken inside the blossoming tulip.
He describes the snapdragon with its little sconce of dew.
He moves from the desk to a window. Remembers his studies
In medicine, picturing the sticky
Overlapping eyelids of drowned children. On the corner
Of the sofa wrapped in Empress-silks there's a box
Of fresh chocolates. He mimics the deceptively distant,
Chittering birdsong within the cat's throat.
How it attracts finches to her open window.
He turns toward the fire, now thinking of late sessions in Storting.
Ibsen had written earlier of an emotional girl
With sunburnt shoulders,

Her surprise when the heavy dipper came up
From the well with frogs' eggs bobbing in her water.
He smiles,

Crosses the room like the fox walking away
From the woodpile.
He picks up his lamp and takes it
To the soft chair beneath the window. Brandy is poured.
Weary, he closes his eyes and dreams
Of his mother at a loom, how she would dip, dressing
The warp with a handful of coarse wool.

Henrik reaches for tobacco — tomorrow, he'll write
Of summer once more, he'll begin with a fragrance…
Now, though, he wonders about the long
Devotion of his muscles to his bones, he's worried by
The wind which hurries the pages in this drafty room.
He looks out
Into the March storm for an illustration: under a tree
A large frozen hare swings at the end of a snare-string.
The fox sits beneath it, his upturned head swinging with it,
The jaws are locked in concentration,

As if the dead hare were soon to awaken.

Comes Winter, the Sea Hunting

for my daughter

This was your very first wall, your crib against
The wall that was papered in a soft
Fawn-color, the powdered wings of a moth
Slowing in the cobwebs of the window —

The moth, poor like us, died
In her paper dress on stilts. The spider
Is a monarch, fat in
Winter chambers, the articles of her
Wealth are also
The articles of the kill: a little narcotic with silk!

We had two rooms in a blue, collapsing roadhouse
At the very lip of a valley
With a deep river and woods. The house
Had been settling for a century.
Those dizzying, tin
Trapezoid rooms…
A house built on rock, a rock built on sand,

And while I slept, your mother, who was
Big with you, hammered from silver —

A knife! A spoon! You,
On a crescent of bone, sleep
A sleep of plums: moisture on the plum forms a window

And inside everything reclines tasting meat and wine
From midday
Until evening. *That winter came in terms of you…*

The wet pods on sticks, mimes playing
Dice in a blizzard! Out of fields of rice come women

From the North, dark pajamas full of explosives...
Your mother now is
Naked and dreaming in the corner,
Is the Elder Brueghel's inverted, golden doe
On a green pole, being
Shouldered back to the winter village.

Inside a box by the stairs there's an egg
Halved by a hair,
A box filled with sleep, and even the retired ferryman,
George Sharon, leaving
Us two bottles of milk in the morning,
Would not look into it!
The cedar balcony in the back took its weight

In ice — first, three large icicles, then five,
And finally a webbing in between of thin ice.
The balcony was sealed
In a wall of crystals. With your new spoon
I carved into this blue-green wall

Dürer's *sky map*
Of the Northern Hemisphere: the silver, ancestral
Figures of crab, spectacle bear,
And *Boötes* with his long pink muscles and spear:

On clear nights the opaque stars above Montpelier
Appeared through this sky chart.

Up in the corner, where
"The fish with spilled pitcher" should be,
There was instead
A bat, snow had
Brought the roof in on him and he was
Caught in ice, hanging by a claw in the eaves.

I called him
Pipistrelle, old and dead flittermouse, he was
A reach of bone and a square of fur like a squirrel
Nailed out on a red barn in October. Pipistrelle,
At the corners of his wings, had blackened stars. Valiant

Dürer's sky map
Was now different with these triangular ears—
The dead pipistrelle carries a sound picture
That is like our memory of the dark trees, or the spaces
Between the old ferryman's teeth.
The bat would use its wings
Like oars; rowing in the blackish cataracts
Of a winter porch: star-room! Lamp-room…

The winter comes,

A sea hunting, and your father after sleeping
Puts his fist into the star wall, making a hole;
The wind entered

Moving at the height of the unborn,
This wind erased the lights of hemispheres!
That night, a breaking of ice, and the next morning
The bag-of-waters begins seeping as your
Mother tries a flight of stairs—

An old woman puts a horn to her stomach, and
Listens for you;

You have formed from seawater:
A deep luminous eye, digits, a bridge for a nose—
Abstract, monstrous—you have two oars!
You can only hear the ferryman in the cove,
Walking with his ladder, he somehow hangs his lamp
On the tall pole.

In an earlier season,

You were conceived, touched by two sounds of water
In a gulf; you formed your pulse, little patch over nothing,

Drawn in and drawn out — this is the meaning as,
Sadly and much later, a feather
Or candle is put to our mouths!

There were
Agates on the windowsill and a vase of dry pussywillows;

The outlarged mapmaker's instruments boiling
Before labor, the towels and basins:
A hatching
In the ruby rhomboidal rooms where

A spider on her lucent thread
Swings into sunlight, then leaves us
Climbing up a silken helix to eaves and

Pigeon gloom, but

You have washed up in the surf, and look out over
A new light like water showing,
Another mother,

A first attempt for someone loved, as
Out of her dress dropped in a circle — this nude,
The steady specter at your birth,
Steps near to kiss you, circle of goldsmith's blue;
The pipistrelles fan the air...
This world would deceive us

So live in it as two! This was the very first wall
                    that you had to have passed through...

Double Sphere, Cloven Sphere

The black clouds swell up around the setting sun
Making a distant elm conspicuous,
Its rosy domination like the claw

On a garden rake held up
Before the face and through which
The blinking leaf fires of late autumn play.

The blue sheaves
Of tree shadows fall across the doorway where
A man and a woman are speaking, looking at their feet,
In the yard full of leaves.

He repeats a simple sentence. The long sleeves
Of her gray sweater will swallow her hands
As she dances a little in place, cold and impatient!

But they are both in pain.

A wet December day has made their naked bodies linger
Like red berries in the memory.

It ends over white papers with a stranger
Who awards the man two chairs, who awards the woman
A sofa and mirror.

They begin to walk away, in opposite directions,
Kicking up leaves — tears down their faces…

This farewell was both simple and difficult.
The incalculable
Ditches in the field below their cold house
Are touched with mist; ice

Forms in the stubble. *These were our times.*

And the slumbering ruse of early winter
Points a long finger in the direction
Of our exile:
            a passage that's all so clear
Taking us over the horizon into atmosphere.

The Composer's Winter Dream

for my father

Vivid and heavy, he strolls through dark brick kitchens
Within the great house of Esterhazy:
A deaf servant's candle
Is tipped toward bakers who are quarreling about
The green kindling! The wassail is
Being made by pouring beer and sherry from dusty bottles

Over thirty baked apples in a large bowl: into
The wassail, young girls empty their aprons of
Cinnamon, ground mace, and allspice berries. A cook adds
Egg whites and brandy. The giant glass snifters
On a silver tray are taken from the kitchens by two maids.
The anxious pianist eats the edges of a fig

Stuffed with Devonshire cream. In the sinks the gallbladders
Of geese are soaking in cold salted water.
Walking in the storm, this evening, he passed
Children in rags, singing carols; they were roped together
In the drifting snow outside the palace gate.
He knew he would remember those boys' faces…

There's a procession into the kitchens: larger boys, each
With a heavy shoe of coal. The pianist sits and looks
Hard at a long black sausage. He will not eat

Before playing the new sonata. Beside him
The table sags with hams, kidney pies, and two shoulders
Of lamb. *A hand rings a bell in the parlor!*

No longer able to hide, he walks
Straight into the large room that blinds him with light.

He sits before the piano still thinking of hulled berries...
The simple sonata which

He is playing has little
To do with what he's feeling: something larger
Where a viola builds, in air, an infinite staircase.
An oboe joins the viola, they struggle
For a more florid harmony.
But the silent violins now emerge

And, like the big wing of a bird, smother everything
In a darkness from which only a single horn escapes —
That feels effaced by the composer's dream...
But he is not dreaming,
The composer is finishing two performances simultaneously!

He is back in the dark kitchens, sulking and counting
His few florins — they have paid him
With a snuffbox that was pressed
With two diamonds, in Holland!
This century discovers quinine.
And the sketchbooks of a mad, sad musician

Who threw a lantern at his landlord who was standing beside
A critic. He screamed: *Here, take the snuffbox, I've filled
It with the dander of dragons!* He apologizes
The next morning, instructing the landlord to take
This *stuff* (Da Ist Der Wisch) to a publisher,
And sell it! *You'll have your velvet garters, Pig!*

The composer is deaf, loud, and feverish... he went
To the countryside in a wet sedan chair.
He said to himself: for the piper, seventy ducats! He'd curse
While running his fingers through his tousled hair, he made
The poor viola climb the stairs.
He desired loquats, loquats with small pears!

Ludwig, there are Spring bears under the pepper trees!
The picnic by the stone house… the minnows
Could have been sunlight striking fissures
In the stream; Ludwig, where your feet are
In the cold stream
Everything is horizontal like the land and living.

The stream saying, "In the beginning was the word
And without the word
Was not anything made that was made…
But let us believe in the word, Ludwig,
For it is like the sea grasses
Off which the giant snails eat, at twilight!" But then

The dream turns to autumn; the tinctures he
Swallows are doing nothing for him, and he shows
The physicians his spoon which has dissolved
In the mixtures the chemist has given him!
After the sonata was heard: the standing for applause
Over, he walked out where it was snowing.

It had been dark early that evening. It's here that the
Dream becomes shocking: he sees a doctor
In white sleeves
Who is sawing at the temporal bones of his ears. There is
A bag of dampened plaster for the death mask. And
Though he *is* dead, a pool of urine runs to the

Middle of the sickroom. A brass urinal is on the floor, it is
The shape of his ears rusting on gauze. The doctors

Drink stale wassail. They frown over the dead Beethoven. Outside,
The same March storm that swept through Vienna an hour before
Has turned in its tracks like the black, caged panther
On exhibit in the Esterhazys' candlelit ballroom. The storm crosses
Over Vienna once more: lightning strikes the Opera House, its eaves
And awnings filled with hailstones,

Flames leaping to the adjacent stables! Someone had known,
As thunder dropped flower boxes off windowsills,
Someone *must* have known
That, at this moment, the violins would emerge
In a struggle with the loud, combatant horns.

The Night Before Thanksgiving

A grove of deep sycamores drifts into the Hudson,
The blue lights on a sledge
Go white as it drags its iron nets
Slowly up the trench of the river:
Inside an old Studebaker, my father sits beside a meadow.
Next to him there's a hot thermos, and a little box
Of codeine tablets for the pain in his knee. He reaches
Over into the backseat for a red plaid blanket; it has
White hair on it from a long-dead cat. The blanket

Goes over his lap — at that moment, a giant
Spectacle moth settles like a falling hazel leaf on the blanket:
The moth, powdered in lime and chalk, has a lurid green
Eye on each forewing: it has come to my father after
A long season of feeding
From the night-flowering sweet tobacco!
The spectacle moth has settled and died, and there is
The smell of burning gasoline.
                                        On the river, a horn blows
Twice from a lamp-room that is followed by barges loaded
With coal; flames from a foundry climb over pine trees that
Are miles down the road...
Across the water there are lanterns
Over the lawns of a mansion where women

In long gowns are playing croquet without wickets. These women
Are drinking; they laugh and wave to
The lonely, bored man in the tugboat who pulls on the horn again.
My father waves to him; the moth closes
Its shattered ice-green eyes like a blackened coal miner
Stepping out of a mountain into winter daylight.

Ode to the Spectral Thief, Alpha

The stream silent as if empty. Dusk in the
mirrors. Doors shutting.
Only one woman without a pitcher remains
in the garden —
Made of water, transparent in moonlight, a
flower in her hair!

YANNIS RITSOS

The way grapes will cast a green rail,
With tendrils and flowers, out along
A broken fence, down the edge of a field,
Then, climbing over hawthorn and up
Into the low branches of an elm. The moon

Is also up in the branches of the elm along with
A raccoon who sits and fills himself
On the dark, dusty fruit—under the branch,
On which the raccoon is situated,
His deep brown feces splatter over
Queen Anne's lace and the waving sedge
Of the pond...

An owl lifts out of the tufted solitary orchard
And there are hot-silver zigzags, lightning
Up in the fat black clouds; this quiet
Before an August storm is nothing at all
Compared to the calm after a snowfall...
But the long boxes of hay in the field
Will stand, they are dense coffins
In which small living things

Are caught, broken: mouse, grasshopper,
And the lame sparrow. The field looks down
To an old quarry and road, and across

To a dark beach on the Atlantic.
Stone from the quarry built a small
Custom's House out on the Point.
Its old form is in ruin, now! But bells are
Still heard out there just before dawn:
Their purpose must fade over the water...

The water knows the three formal elements
That should compose an ode: say it, *élan!*
There's turn and counterturn...
And turn, again; not *stand!*
The epode has a talent for rattling a tambourine
Like pie tins strung across a garden
To frighten, at night, the subtle, foraging deer.

The epode knows about fear; but, shaking
In its bones, I've said it has a talent for
Playing the tambourine by ear.
The raccoon struggling out of his tree
Doesn't care about
The eye, bait, and teeth of a Windsor Trap;
The pie tins, touched by a wind moving
Over the spears of corn, do not

Confuse him.
He wanders off into the orchard and down
Into a fast stream where suddenly
A grinning hound stops him —
The coon rears up on his haunches like a bear,
Spits and screams: his claws
Tear at the weeping eyes of the big dog: turned twice,

The hound bites into fur, meat, and *then*
Deep into the spilled milk of the spine. This is
When the stream seems empty, silent!
This is also where the story divides in my mind.
What can I tell you?

Only that in past centuries
There were fewer
Dimensions to any concept of time,
And there was a greater acceptance of mirrors, and rhyme.

The Parallax Monograph for Rodin

I dreamt, last night, of your stone cabinet, *Porte de l'Enfer,*
Everything was there, except it had turned into
The doors of an elevator in an old hotel of potted ferns. I'm certain
That outside the hotel there was a beach with, here and there,
                a colorful
But faded umbrella! I said it wasn't changed, but that's not fair;
I hesitate to say this but *the contemplative,* with his head
Resting on his fist, was replaced, in the dream, by a clock
That somehow told the time of day and the location of the elevator!
The face of all this work seemed unchanged, still a clamoring
Of naked men and women, not religious but ordered
In their desperation.

My favorite figure remains: the woman on the far right just below
The strong backside of a man who's assisted in his climb: his left foot
Lifts from her extended left hand and arm — her hair cannot be
Described, omitted as if swept aside by a severe comb,
Her breast is young but not exactly firm.
I don't really know if she assists
The man above her or if this was just an opportunity he seized;
After all, his right foot rests on a head that has no body.
I sense their community as being *of oblivion.* Outside
This hotel elevator the unbaptized infants wait, unwashed and
Smoking green cigars, they are delayed, in limbo...

The dream has worked a parody of your dark, portal scene,
Deus ex machina, and your intense belief in a teeming life

That struggles for relief out of a slab of rock in which
You saw it all from the very beginning: helmets, wings, thighs,
Breasts, hands, ankles, mouths, and even the small cherub peeing
Into the cracked mirror. The mirror is the mouth of an obese banker
From Reims. Everything you made

Was placed in an enclosing but not final space. Only the most
Brilliant comedian possesses your gestures in their correct
Abstract mathematical sequence. I think by now

We must be alone!
My bored reader having left us both for a fresh lettuce sandwich —
Sometimes abstraction suits me like throwing rocks
In a building with a simple clerestory of stained glass. *We should
Discuss light.* It has suggestive, serial properties like a girl's loud
Orgasm in a drifting rowboat over a peaceful river, at night.
Let's pretend the lovers in the rowboat have drifted for nearly
A kilometer, and now, at the moment that she announces
Her arrival at this thunderstruck height, her lover discovers
They have floated up to a dock filled with aristocrats
At a party with lapdogs, wine, and hanging lanterns…

The girl is sitting on the boy, the rowboat rocks gently.
The boy's nakedness is lost, made modest, by his partner's
Large thighs and buttocks, she
Is indifferent to the strangers on the dock; she goes on
Screaming the boy's name, and the rowboat drifts past,
Back into the shadows of the trees that contain the river.
Wonderful! The aristocrats are bent in stitches of laughter.

I was talking about your comical gestures, and an obscure thought
That discouraged my reader, who left for a sandwich. To punish
Him I have invented this charming vignette of pleasure
Which he's missed!
He thinks little of your materials: there's strings, wires, planes, and
Cubes. The vertical sequences of nudes. You appraised a nude
Like a sturdy chair or stool.

The way you place Balzac's head in that massive unfinished neck,
His face is like a smashed gem in matrix.
The apprehension of chiaroscuro, as in the lines of a daffodil, is
Not your style. The princess, David, of Donatello is not your style!
Anything freestanding like a glutton in an English garden *is*
Your style.

The infants, unwashed, still smoking cigars, in front of your elevator,
Have begun a card game; they curse and spit but are not offensive.

Rodin, I've put off saying this, but your male secretary is sad
And disheartened...
He writes with power about the corpse on the kitchen table.
In triplicate, he's sent an application, listing grievances, to the stars!
He now operates your old elevator in that dream hotel.
He's left everyone in the lurch; ground level. What's he doing now
That instructs the summer guests to undress and climb the walls?
Tortured and naked, they seem to have little patience with him.
His name? The real key is silver on a chain streaming from his pocket.

Your secretary is on the roof of the hotel having a smoke
While looking out over the ocean. He has been joined by two waiters.
They gaze out over the water, remembering the quiet
Days of the winter. You were smart
To have a poet as your servant in serious matters.
And what's more important than this closet on a string, the box that
Climbs vertically through the large, broken-down hotel, famous
For its spirits of bottled water! One of the two
Waiters finishing his smoke becomes careless...
There are screams of *Fire, Fire!* My faithless reader
Done with his sandwich, and a lover of big fires, returns
And says: *What an inferno, they are all lost; poor souls!*
I have not guessed the secrets of your closet. But out on the Atlantic

A ship bobs up and down, a sailor
Looks over to land and sees the burning parallax beams of the hotel.

The sailor's brow is like marble... my reader in a trembling voice
Speaks to the sailor, asking, "What's the matter, what's that
Fire on the shore?" The sailor answers,

"It's Hell, of course."

The World Isn't a Wedding of the Artists of Yesterday

A stub of a red pencil in your hand.

A Georgia O'Keeffe landscape rising beyond
The carcass of black larkspur,
Beyond the Milky Way where
The lights of galaxies are strung out over a dipper of gin
With a large sun and the rotund

Fuchsia moon. Her closet is empty, except for the manuscript
With your signature. She has left you!
Where was it in the field
That you threw the telephone:
After moving away
From the farmhouse, you found it again when
Returning for the lost cat —

As you walked through the low chinaberries calling
Her name you found the white horn
Of the telephone. You are alone calling to the frozen
Countryside of New Jersey.
She sleeps
In the yellow wicks of the meadow:
You are calling the mopsy cat back

From the ditch, but Dexedrine presses a pencil
Up against your eyebrow and temple. And
You've forgotten — *what was it?*
Out there in the field calling

Across the cold night air, drinking from the gold flask,
Again tucking that stub of a pencil
Back behind your ear. You read, this morning,
In the crisp pica lettering of the old Remington
How boatmen navigated the winter shallows of the Seine
Guided by a lamp burning all night
In a narrow window in Flaubert's study;

And all of a sudden, under severe stars, beside water,
You remembered everyone who was a friend.

But why your hand is locked on a red pencil, again,
At the bottom of a wintry meadow, in New Jersey,

Is a mystery rising behind you on the wind.

The Scrivener's Roses

for Marvin Fisher

The gulls fly in close formation becoming a patch of sail...
They divide revealing a blue patch of sky. They dive
At a gun carriage on which the dead cot-boy writhed
Much of last night. It is a flight of seagulls
Above the drying cannon brooms that makes the bay
Seem at all alive. It is over the dead water that the surgeons
Come:
                               over the bay American ships of war give up
Their cutters, the handsome surgeons climbing
Into rowboats and transported to the flagship where
The Surgeon of the Fleet chews patiently on beefsteak
Within this dark, dry man-of-war.
They will gather for an amputation:
On dressers an orderly arranges saws and knives, sponges
And tincture of iodine, the hooked darning needles are beside
The yellow beeswax and thread. One boy is dead, another
Is barely alive. The oldest surgeon's face
Is white with scarlet brands like the ash hole in sick bay
With its few *live* red coals in a deep pan. The sawing on
The mahogany femur of the thigh is trying for the aging physician.
The leg will be hidden from sight behind a woodpile.
Across the bay on the beach a dark flamingo, in ridicule, stands
On just one leg. And a bugle signals
The return of the cutters to their separate ships.

The two dead boys are from New England. What had they endured?
They often said that an April snow was a poor man's manure.
Their sisters work in Carson's Old Paper Mill. The youngest girl
Worked a Tymer press, an iron machine that drops a weighted, sunken
Impression of roses onto a soft, scented stationery.
Two of the sisters have died in the mill, mauled by machinery!

The sleighs that are usually loaded with paper carried their bodies to
The cemetery on the hill.

Their distant cousin, Herman Melville, attended both burials.
He said to their mother, "Ruth, you still have a husband, two boys
At sea, and Elizabeth who'll soon marry. That baker's stove
The girls gave to me flared up last week, scorching my study window.
The window now is like a Claude glass; it frames
The river and snowy fields
While giving them the golden lights of the Claude Lorrain landscape.
I'll remember the girls each time I stare through the panes
Of that almost amber window!"

Leaving his cousins, Melville on a train studies a passing meadow:
He has never before seen jacks-in-the-pulpit flowering
In snow, standing in a late-spring snow! He felt that the meadow
Was a white necropolis with toppled towers like halves of eggshells
After the weasel has raided the henhouse.
He wondered were black ants dead inside the walls
Of this wide, tufted city? He longed for the hearth.
For cider bottles popping in the cellar. For muffins with honey!

He will visit a small branch of The Dead Letter Office in Washington:
A large house with bare rooms, five rooms in the round, and
Each has a fireplace leading to a common, federal chimney. Five clerks
Wrapped in scarves stand before their assigned fire. They open
The letters spilling coins and rings into a steamer trunk. There are
The thin silver rings for children; rings of engagement for fingers

Already tattered to the bone like masts of a ghost ship
Under an opaque moon. These letters
Spoke of affection, luck fishing for trout, of drought, of the deaths
Of this and that rich uncle. Five clerks at each fire, five fires! The black

Smoke rises from the single great stack, and a shopgirl across
The street in her attic room writes a letter describing
The smoke as it drifts

Out over Washington to the bay and woods. She writes
On scented sheets
To her brother who is at sea. He died in February. She is run over
That evening by a wagon loaded with raw cotton. Herman Melville
        stood
Over her in the street.
Just above her blue stocking, above
The blue garter
Is a wound in her thigh and a spurting artery, horse manure
And young active flies...

Walking back to the hotel he decides to return to his home by Friday,
He'll sit on the north porch and write and heal, the north porch
Like a sleety deck of a ship where the Captain is lashed to the wheel...

That Appius Claudius failed to drain the Pontine Marshes is similar,
He believes, to this government's failure to burn all the dead letters
Of just a single week! He feels they could simply be scattered like gulls
        from the crow's nests of ships out on the open sea!

The convent is in ruin. The churchyard is a basin filled with graves and
It extends into the adjacent park where farmers are chopping down trees
So as to be able to dig more graves late that evening. Sherman's artillery
Has destroyed the joists and center beam of
The convent, killing fifty-three nuns and an old priest. The farmers cut

Down trees and the birds and red squirrels are fleeing to the stream that
Is beside the old Saw Mill and its livery...
The next afternoon the Union soldiers enter the town,
They lose the light

Of day while looting and drinking. At dusk, searching for women, they
Arrive at the churchyard—with bayonets they open the fresh mounds
Where the sisters were hurriedly buried. Lanterns are strung up
In the few standing trees, the cook plays his red accordion, and

The men in their blue caps and jackets are dancing clumsily with
The dead women who have been stripped to the waist; their white bibs
And black birdcloth veils littering the green bowl
Of the dim churchyard:
Out of the mouths of the jostled corpses falls grave soil and
Ivory crowns from teeth. The dancing soldiers are laughing
With their rigid partners in moonlight — you can hear dry bones
Breaking! Some of the women are shaven, one has long red hair.
Their white breasts bouncing in the chill night air. Behind the hedge
Of the churchyard three black children hide while sobbing.
They understand these free men grinning through beards,
Drinking whiskey; one falling back into an empty grave.
Two sergeants, who are yet boys, are undressing the gray-haired
Mother Superior...

In this judgment the dead climb out of their shallow places
And waltz — all but three are now completely naked!
There are halos of cigar smoke over the struggling couples.
The nun with red hair is young and freckled with a bloodless bayonet
Wound in her neck. One of her eyes is bruised shut; the other is
Open, ice-green and resigned. A bonfire is started.

You can hear hammers striking rail down by the depot.

The severe ebony-and-pearl garments of the sisters are thrown
On the fire. And what we know

Is that in the morning these soldiers, in a line three-deep,
Moved on through Georgia for the sea...

———————

The Chinese creeper climbing over lilac beside the piazza
Is infested with worms. The swing
On the piazza is nudged by wind, and Melville
Empties his pipe against the stone drain.

On the porch, at sunset, he trembles a little
Both in act and shadow,

Memento mori... the Antigone of paper, who dropped her sweet, iron
Roses onto thin polished sheets; but her sister, Elizabeth,
Is alive and has
Written from Washington to their brothers, the sailors;

They have been buried in a tropical cemetery for paupers and pilgrims.
Elizabeth has accidentally rented a room across
From the house to which her letter will be delivered.
She has told her brothers there will not be civil war.
She enclosed a watercolor miniature that depicts nuns bent in labor
In a sunny cotton field in Georgia.
And up the federal chimney goes this gesture of an ordinary, occult
Shopgirl. The genius of her vigil mixes ashes with ashes,
Tears with tears, and ink with the long white fabric of paper...

A fisherman
Out at sea held a packet of seeds and wished he'd hear
The madness of roosters as he neared the land and long beaches.
The winter beaches with their snowy dunes, white on white, or

Memento mori... the crisp depression of a clear rose
On its clear stem. This perfumed impression
In the corner of a crème paper
Is our lesson in understanding him: Melville dreamed he was

At sea in a state cabin which was sealed and caulked for an eternal
Crossing of the Atlantic. There are mice
In the desk drawers. Dust everywhere. And large linens
Draped over the furniture and mirrors.
It was like the mystery of a yellow scroll.
It was losing your soul down the awful mouth of a newborn, the perfect
Mouth spitting breast milk, while the infant in coarse swaddling
Is bricked up
                              inside the convent's south garden wall.

The Circus Ringmaster's Apology to God

It is what we both knew in the sunlight of a restaurant's garden
As we drank too much and touched
While waiting for the lemon wedges and rainbow trout.
If it's about that door? I'm not sorry.
You smiled through tears. The night clerk said that I was
Crazy like a bear. Laughing, you spilled your beer.

Over the hedge a farmer paints a horse's cankers
With a heavy tincture of violet...

Later, in a dark room, both of us speckled, middle-aged, and soft,
I dragged my mouth like a snail's foot up your leg and body
To your mouth. We both shivered.
You ran naked before a window. Shyness increases your importance!

I don't know what you think when we are no one for a moment:
Hay-ropes, hands at ankles, gone beyond
Even the dripping faucet and its sink spilling onto the floor...

There's no strongbox hidden in the closet.

It's often like laughter, "You go pee for me and I'll boil the water."
Sipping hot coffee, you told me a story about the old ringmaster
On the Baltic shore:
                    he's inside his little house on wheels, and
The goldfinch jumps from its silver platform to the cage's floor
That's littered with straw and shredded handbills. The ringmaster
            daydreams
About ponies circling in a white path of ashes...
On the table before him there's an ounce of tobacco
And in his plate: blue and gray parsnips, beef and the opened letter

That he knows better than the loose floorboard! The two of us
Enjoy our solitude:
>   folded over chairs are the clothes

We never wore. If you die first, I'll sway in the hallway like a bear.
>   I'll whisper, "I'm sorry." And you'll
Not unlock the door.
I'll break through with my hip and shoulder...
Remember? You were glad that I did it once before!

Coleridge Crossing the Plain of Jars

The Gypsies carry sacks of walnuts out of the groves.
A dog
Whimpers below the cemetery, near to the peat field.

With regard to color primarily, but also
Scent and form,
The browsing deer under the sycamores
Have the very properties of a peach
Spoiled on the branch by a blanketing frost...

The deer, in Asia,
Rise out of fog as though it were a pond.

I walk. And over the wind, I hear the crushing
Of talc for the shaping of a death mask. Why is it?

Young Keats is lost!

Joseph Severn's hurried sketch of the rouged corpse
Was like that deep violet thumbprint, this morning,
In the soft breast of a goose
Hung in the draughty printshop of my publisher!

Sara watched from her window above the philodendron
While I crossed against the West Wind
Through the drifting snow. She lost sight of me
For a moment. She guessed I was again wrestling
The angel.
I did die there, briefly, in the blizzard
As I had once with my mother as a boy—
The first of April, nude except for our canvas shoes,
We stepped
Under the bitter waterfall fed with a runoff of snow.

My brain empties

As it will when I've stood under the compass
Of a great low chandelier, weighted
In the purity
Of vertical tiers of burning citron candles.

The Gypsies' bonfire climbs the stone face
Of the nunnery.
A Christmas pie, already sampled by the children,

Sits on the cleared table.
I stepped into the parlor, and Sara said, "I thought
The elements had swallowed you
Just as you passed the last sycamore?"

She smiled in her chair, from half-dark,
And sewed—
I knew the chipped fire of pond ice
Was in her eyes like a widow's soul.

Principia Mathematica: Einstein's Exile in an Old Dutch Winter

My theory withstood the light of the Hyades

While it passed our darkened sun. The eclipse
Was captured in Brazil and west Africa.
Here, at night, over the fields
The straightedge and compass become the severe poplar
And snowy tar-tipped spruce of Holland.
At this hour, I miss Berlin!
Descartes, too, once sat here washing oysters in milk,
The oysters of Leyden,
Laying them out over a bowl of snow,
Sprinkling pepper
Into the milk in its deep saucer,

A young mathematician
At the interior
Of a silver and gold mirror filled
With a watercolorist's impression
Of smokefall in winter.

There exists an imaginary plane, made
Increasingly solid with distance,
Like the weathered mechanical wings

Of a windmill, four pine blades
Becoming eight, becoming a bald porcelain face
In the amethyst shade
Of a cloudbank passing between sun
And the broken reeds of the lake.

Outside Leyden,
The wind is the lamp of projection!

Descartes, wintering with the armies
Of the Duke of Savoy, sat in his large furs
On the blazing bank of the Danube
Lecturing young bowmen, crying
That all of the pleasure of mathematics
Was in the one smooth pebble of *the calculus.*

There exists a flower, in Holland,
Which is not a member
Of the tremendous family of roses —
A flower which *is,* regardless,
The rose of all roses...

When the arrow passed through the fist
Of Cardinal Richelieu, he was dressed
In the red glove of his office; we would have said
His wound was discrete
And continuous
Like the brown burn of a canker on a rosebud.
My son has suffered a nervous breakdown!

He and I watched, in Venice, beside the old *Coq d'Or* —
In the vast relief of an exotic poverty, a barge's
Cargo of poppies was sucked down
Making sentient a geometry of water. I dreamt
Later of this vortex, in Pasadena,
In a closing circle which grew smaller,

More concentrated, until all the flowers
Fell through the bottom of their concentration
Opening into a Siamese twin: two cones, black
Shifted to red, of infinite dimension —

If I enter myself with all the dignity
Of nature I will never come out again.

Descartes, in the windmill, grabbed linen
And a tarnished mothy spoon,
Sipped his peppered milk, studying himself
In the deep-running mirror...

First light will enter his room like the powder-blue
Lepidoptera of spring, come
To visit the mathematician
Who'll, now, sleep until evening dreaming
The triadic stream where
The opened breastbone of a swan
With its pier-and-lintel bones is like the window
Which contains the wintry reflection
Of the setting sun:

A waking Descartes, his red beard and smock,
Gazes out of the inferno of his window—
He is thinking of the transformative nature
Of light and symbol, he proposes

That the wasp nest up in the eaves on the windmill
Resembles the dead blossom on the lilac hedge.
Descartes is waking, he remembers the woes,
And the downcast eyes
Of his dear friend, the exiled Princess Elizabeth—
Again, in flight from emotion, he proposes...

The rose of all roses!

Lord Myth

A shadow through the room, a rising
Fan of violets, phenomenon
With scent, weighted with one Victorian

Iris: her long finger passes
Through the velvet drawer
Where the children's salt crystals
Are seeding along soft black threads.

In moving candlelight, still solemn,
She turns to him
And with the effort of a faint pilgrim,

At twilight, opening great barn doors,
He opens her robe. She turns, he moans. There's

A rill of breast milk, a sudden sequence
Magically appearing in the deep specimen drawer.

The raven above her, on top of the oak breakfront,
Flies across the room, dragging its long tether
To the arm of the sofa. She is silent.
He whimpers.

The marble andirons cool and snap—
A pulse in the fat red crest between them.
The sun
Has set between the cliffs: inland,
And hounds are chasing something
Big across a wet sloping lawn…

The raven's descent to the sofa
Snuffed the storm-candle, carbon
Spackling the high ceiling above her—

A black feather plunges through the spiraling smoke.

Not the Cuckold's Dream

for Sam Pereira

He lifts the white skiff up onto the beach. It is Easter.
He hears the tin bells of the peninsula. A storm coming?
Two torches smudge, then,
In the blue night, burn cleanly again...
The pearl slapdash of the moon

Is on the water. He lifts a flying fish
By its pink underwing, hurriedly snipping
With his teeth the last blood-blisters
Like a string of peppers ripe across his fingers.

At the rope ladder, he pauses and sits on the cold sand
To rub life into his feet.
He rinses his infected hands in the fire of bound cattails.

The fisherman touches the ladder of maguey flesh, and
Pulls up!
Swaying, he is like a gull's shadow
Climbing on thermals before the white cliff. The tide

Will follow behind him; rising in storm
It shatters the long skiff against the red adobe henhouse.

His strong, dark wife, a giantess, thought it was personal.
She comes out waving, in hysteria, a handkerchief.
She loses her laughter to a stitch. The wind taken from her:

She is knocked back and then down
By the falling water. The heavy pleated dress

Washes over her ashen face. She wishes
She had learned to swim.
There is a feeling of needles in her legs. He told

Her about the sea. *The sea is always feeding.*
The blood of his blistered hands is in his hair.
The fisherman raises dry bread to his mouth.

If I do not drown, *he thought of the father,*
I will marry, *he thought of the fish…*

After Spring Snow, What They Saw

There are thirty-six folds to nothing—
Picture a holy man being eaten by two tigers.
The lovers are one white candle of procession
Descending the terraces of the winter garden.
She opens her mouth to the snowfall.
His knee
Is blue against her shadowed breast.
She arches her back
Grasping the pillow
And in the continuous light
Deer clatter past her, swerve
Up the rocks to the gorge...

His mouth, also, is open to darkness
While the large star-polyhedra
Of a cold interior
Float down over the two lovers
Like individual snowflakes into black water.
A rabbit scurries
And snow drops from the bough, a snare
Of juniper berries startling the cows,
The naked young couple
Are watched by an owl in a tree.
The man is weighted.
Across the axis of the bed, one candle
Of procession brushing him
Under the spidery, marble pendentives...
Red maple leaves
Rush from a tree like blood
Leaving the charred muscle that stops
First in her, first in him!

Rats circle over the translucent panels
Of the ceiling...
An archer in a big hood stands
With his back to falling water, the rail
Of his crossbow
Slamming back against his chest,
Which shallows, releasing its held breath:
The arrow recedes
Past its vanishing point in the icy falls.

There are large mirrors, half-buried
In the snow: in summer, they collect dew.
The mirrors are concave sheets of pink mica,
Burnished glass, or jagged silver meteorites
Gathered over the generations.
This is the night of the great snail
Who has buried itself under decayed leaves
And black soil; painfully, months ago,
It dragged in its toe and heavy lime capstone.

The dead in their mud houses below the gorge
Sleep in the cinnabar stream
Of a winding sheet. They know
Her warm tears flow over his mouth, flowing
Into the hollows of her shoulders
And down over the frozen stepped stones

Of the enchanted garden where the russet hood
Of the poacher
Is visible, then, is not.
The owl thought
The young couple from above
Were like the poacher's dozen caged doves —
Wild inscribable wings attempting flight
Or, like the couple, love...

The Everlastings

for L.P. Snyder and Karma Wangmo

In the village it must be a clear night with the light of a red
Star twisting down the water
Filling the distant mouth of our narrow fjord...

Snow blankets the sleeping mustard, thistle, and gorse!

Two longships have been brought up on forms:
Their bellies are checkered with tar and goatskins.
The wind is up in the bones. The dogs
Are peaceful. I have died
On a beach in France. A monk
And I did battle. I wish I could burn the little icon
Of the nut-fairy; its red berries in the triangular seed-box
And the roof of furze and maple. It was a gift
From the King, my father. Tonight, here in the water I feel
Closer to my mother...

       In the frescoes
       Of the lives of the saints, there's hibiscus, rhubarb,
       And roses sketched on wet plaster, each flower
       Outlined by a fine bone pencil, and when the lime

       Touches the air the watercolors
       Become thin, speckled —
       A daubing of light

In the cobwebs suspended between a stag's antlers.
Saint Odoacer, our fourth pope, brought to the lepers
The fanaticism of the rose
With its old, unfolding characteristics of fire.

He embalmed the Viking's daughter,
Scooping out her breads and heart: in their place
He laid sticks of balsam with salt.
He put spices inside her skull.
He sat her in a jar with the knees snapped, brought back
Under her jaws.

The jar filled with wild, languorous honey!

My stomach is opened. My sword fell at the Viking's collar,
Leaving the body above the silver-braided waist—
Arm and shoulder dropping into the surf.

The moon sits on my shield, lighting the circle
Of oxskulls
Which the goldsmith staggered, every third one, with
Delicately hammered suns...

My daughter's womb was put in an ark of osier and sedge;
Taken out over the waters in a votive ship...
On my shield, at the center of the oxskulls, there is
A silver wreath, all of this worked into its carapace
That is the brine-soaked shell of a sea tortoise. I cracked the Pope's
Skull with it. I have scattered his monks!
I no longer dream of long oars breaking up
In the drifting lakes of kelp. The lodestone,
In its sock of pig intestine, spins to the south? Not Odin
Calling? The fingers of the fog are white like every ninth wave
Across our bow.
My daughter was born in a pine forest in midsummer.

To die at dawn is to wash down with hot ale the raw red livers
Of sea turtles. *Is to smile at my father!* What I feel
Is not fear, it's more the sudden circumspection
Of deer just before they follow the white roebuck who leaps
Over horizons.

HAIL NORTHMAN! HOW IS IT? No, he'll think that
I'm taunting him. He could be free in the tides? There was blood
All over him and sea foam like the saliva of wild dogs.
His beard stood in the sun like laden papers
Of honeycomb. In the lives of the saints there are red stars,
And one is painted over another, crossing out the eyes
Of the unicorn and lion. The Norsemen thought the frescoes
Were secret maps to the Underworld, and they'll voyage anywhere:

They have pulled oars while caught in maelstroms. They filled
Sails while being dragged down into the blood-sworls
Of their thumbs. I love the pandemonium. Listen —

It is the thunder at dawn!

An Old Woman's Vision

No better day to come,
The breath of a worm-soft wind
Lifts me above the hill
Above the narrow road through pine barrens;
I smell Father's flower,
The long blue valerians, they stood
In a round of dark inkweed
And bird's-foot violets. The old skunk,
Midnight, sometimes sat
In that loft of the garden,
Invisible in the stript light of the moon.

The visiting nurse said
My fever would spike after supper; the wind
Lifts and then drags fireflies
In white zigzags, in a child's chalk,
Through night air. There's no chance,
In crossing,
That love will fail. I buried the cat,

Then blood showed in the pail.
A spider sits in his milk plate.
My cat with his snowy neck
Died with a blood blister
On his pink shaved hip and now that the smell
Of dirt is on him
Down in the yellowing underworld
Of bunchgrass, I fall back

And fly to where swamp gas
Rises to light the ditch to the old pond.
Here, all gooseflesh,
My husband waded through the reeds

Then to swim across to me:
The silk belly of a frog, he rose
From the bottom and broke the water
With a sound
Like a sucking stone going down…

Several Measures for the Little Lost

The lesson begins in a heated room
Within a fortified wall of the old town;
Here, hundreds of years earlier, below the darkened window,
Two armies, one blue, one gold,
Crossed through each other in a ruin of mud, cries
Of fallen horses volleying
With muskets and cannon, waterfowl rising...

But, now, the lesson has begun: the mother putting wood
In the porcelain stove,
Her child at the piano dreaming
Of the white charged wings
Of the constellation, *Cassiopeia* —
Last light striking
The oak and brass armillary beside the teacher
Who is eating from a cold leg of lamb.

There is the ordinary compass of a violin
Leaping from the left hand of the prodigy.
The teacher, this early spring,
Wonders why he is thinking
Of a pear-shaped mute of vellum
Being thrust into the bell of a trumpet.
He asks for more mustard on the lamb. The mother
Scurries into an adjoining room...

Equal spaces are being swept out in equal times!

The child is concentrating on the pedals
Moving beneath his trousers, saliva gathering
At the corners of his mouth,
And his foot in its dark slipper
Raises the damper from the wire

So that the final sound may be prolonged
After the child's finger has left the ivory key,
After all of the lamb has left the bone it warmed.

Grandmother

A spider floats from the apple tree
With a silk thread
Through air to the blossoming dogwood.
The long silk,

Spittle and linchpin, is cut
By the wing of an evening grosbeak.

Over the late lawn,
Between flowering trees like blue parallel snowfields,
Is a cedar birdhouse
Within which a man wakes. The cut thread,
A function of silence...

He rises in a renouncing space to a song:
A sharp, double *whit-sweet*.
The corn husks will serve as clothing.
The new light within him passes, incognito,
Down silk like a darkening hall:
In the hours he was visited:

The cloak of nearness, his dead grandmother,
Who speaks, "No more yellow wheat; joint of beef!"

He woke within cedar walls,
She stood beside him and he was quieted
As though no one
Had proved to be there at all.

Pictures at an Exhibition

for Pamela Stewart

It's best, when watching the surprising levitations
Before the great gates of Kiev,
To believe the children are suddenly silent
Because an autumn storm,
                              still distant,
Announces itself through them —
                              they go
To their separate meditations
Like sparrows down to the raw ditch.
The juggler's copper balls
                              are no longer
Gushing from his sleeves. Dwarfs
Are climbing down from one another's shoulders:
The largest of these blue diminutives
                              drops —
An afterthought making him roll
Before the wheels of a hurried cart:
On the other side
                    he springs to his feet, laughing,
And the bells
Hooked on his ears are loudest
Now for him.
Two bearded priests
Stopped their spitting to watch
                              the dwarf's daring somersault.
Black thunderheads are over the eastern towers
Of the city. The grief
                    in this music repeats a dusky scene
For me. *For you I will see what I can see.*
An old troubadour and a red gnome with a damaged leg
Step with a lantern down from the casement

Leaving the catacombs:
                              beyond them the dark castle is barely
Visible in the heavy architectural waters:
                                            the skulls
Are somehow illuminated from within themselves. Why
Is it not possible for us to realize
That all
Of the skulls are grinning in this large generation
Of calcium and light?
                              I am not sorry. I said
That for you
                    I will see what I can see: *all of the dead
Are grinning!*
It is not personal music that believes in *one* soul, or two
Twined

For or against mystery, *this is misery...*
It is why you have left me
                              with the most personal of beliefs
In the one and the many. Mussorgsky's friend, a painter, died
As we must to this and that life.
I will admit I am drinking tonight, hearing the promenade
Of the romantic Mussorgsky, ten notes
                                        crisp as the spade collars
Of the harassed nurses
                        with their charges in the Tuileries.
The children are set to quarreling, sparrows
Dropping to the ditch.
                        All these centuries
We have shared the storms, their beauty
Sweeping through the city, making of the one,
                                              the many.
I will admit the children have stopped quarreling
In the queer yellow light that felled the birds.
All motion is a little arc between two deaths. And if
You think you are justified by light
                              then you have rolled

To your left shoulder, tucked your head,
Smelled,
                ever so briefly, the manure caked
To the huge insides of the thighs of oxen
Who are punished with a birch stick
By a farmer in flight
From the certain promise of rain,
                                    the children strangely silent.
And up you come, again, as if sprung
From the toes
                that take the shock of your landing.
Rain splatters on your open face and hands...
Music is everything!
                                    I admit
The little fists of the dwarf opening in the air
Are reason enough to live,
                        reason enough for Mussorgsky to die
Less than ten years after his friend. I know
Nothing, virtually nothing, of either of them.
                                    But this
Is not the pattern the dwarf left in the air, *unbuckling*
What?
        All those large, fully formed organs
Inside his tiny frame. Maybe? Maybe just our fertile, giant need
To please ourselves,
                who are the many. It was another century
                                            haggling
We so reduce things! Do you see,
                        with time,
How music is everything; even risk,
            set aside like land, will be blessed by rain.

To a Young Woman Dying at Weir

She hears a hermit laughing
Like a great scapegrace of waxwings and crows.
He is laughing about the burdock seed

That is in the horse manure
That is in the sheriff's compost.
Last night, unable to sleep,
She recalled the catbird
Wheezing out in the chinaberry tree.
Soon frost would splatter
Iodine all over the hydrangeas
And the deer would no longer graze
Under the blood maples along the hill.

Sometimes her spirit grows and she remembers
A mountain dulcimer being played
While a woman sews. When the fear is largest
She remembers the old hermit poling his boat
Back along the cooling pond; he's taken burlap bags
Of the whitest sand from the cove
For plastering the walls of his autumn shack:
This comforts her,
                    errand and prospect,
A freshened sense of snow
Feathering over the frozen pond. She says
                    in a hush
That she loves something she has not found.

Penelope

I have looked for you at the familiar center
Of the turning red trees, a few
Alder leaves rising with lustrous
Sheets of rain that change
To green streamers like ivy darkening
The windowpanes...

I have smoothed the earth over a suitor's grave.
The loom sleeps
Having eaten of the shorn path
That crosses under the belly of the lamb...

Once you slept across me,
The big pulse in your thigh
Laid like a coin over the pulse that's down low
On my stomach;

The moon drags the sea
To the chalk shelf of red trees —
And I am bitter about everything, but

The radishes deliver themselves early
To please me; the hard
White peas are sweetening
Among fat mint leaves. The changing

Of the seasons has made sleep easy —
I have watched for the naked stranger, Ulysses,
Who in the dead thesis of voyage, avoids me.

Chemin de Fer

A chapel has fallen into ruins:
The still-standing corners, each with two
Gray triangles
Like stone bathers reclining
On their elbows along a white, windy shore...

This ruin in the meadow was the dominion
Of Francis of Assisi, who tamed
The large wolf. *He dreamt of an iron road,*
And was kind to the hour.
At noon, he said to the turtle

Whatever he had said earlier
To the difficult sparrows in the morning meadow.
He dreams
Of an iron cocoon nesting in fire,
And he was kind to the hour!

His chapel fell into flowers years ago:
Lilies of the valley: you know
That each has a white hood shaped
Like the spout on an old water pump—

Its severed goose-wing of snow.

Hummingbirds

They will be without arms like God.

By the millions their dried skins will be sought
In the new world.
Their young will be like wet slugs.
They will obsess the moon
Over a field of night-flowering phlox.
Their nests will be a delicate cup of moss.

In pairs
They will feast on a tarantula in thin air.

They have made a new statement
About our world — a clerk in Memphis
Has confessed to laying out feeders
Filled with sulfuric acid. She says

God asked for these deaths... like God
They are insignificant, and have visited us

Who are wretched.

Elsinore in the Late Ancient Autumn

for J.

I hear a dead march. A thin wrist is mincing roses
In the diagonal lights of the castle's arbor.
It is the nun at her stone bench.
We need new quantities
Of perfume for our palpable dead!

The landlord is no longer at war. Someone whispers

To me, "Yorick? Yorick?"
There are four gates to the cemetery.
The North Gate opens to the Northwind.
The North Gate closes in the Southwind. As I lie awake,
Past midnight,
I can identify the prevailing wind
By its loud entrance into the churchyard:
According to the season, I can say
What future weather
Comes to Elsinore by calling
The cardinal sequences of gates—four compass points,
By eight voices that creak, each
With individual personality, in the night…

To the West, below the drawbridge,
The dew-mirrored vortices of wolf spiders
Are drying in anise weed. The hourglass nest of a wolf spider
Was copied by me in willow and damask.
From this contrivance the fishermen
Made baskets which collect unguessed weights
Of flounder and sweet sea-bass.
Once, these men desired nothing more
Than the iridescent withers of a strong horse,
A few potatoes, and lasting benefice.

When the Prince's blue foot
Broke into cold space, all spectators went dumb!
The Queen looked to me for strength:
Her Clown returned the anxious inquiry
By whispering, "My Dame, you've swallowed him, we think!"
She silenced me with her cold hand!

From a hanging tree the dressed stag in air
Swayed under a shifting weight of flies,
From the secret place I stole the gamekeeper's
Black wrap of knives. We opened Gertrude,
In the French manner, along her hairline —

There was a peal of ordnance
To announce our Prince, alive and strong! The King
Said a prayer from the checkered parapet
That commands the Sound.
Storied is the world, plotted is the ground.
That's what I sing to the sandy
Dog-pimpernels, in spring, in their new havens...

The night of Prince Hamlet's birth,
It was said,
Worms came up out of the earth
Without a promise of rain to summon them?
I upset the bowl of my warm breath
Over the newborn's mouth and nostrils.
He resented this, I laughed
While the Queen patted him dry with lambskin.

The nun, done chewing at the rosebuds, brought
In for me a cockleshell
To be worn in young Hamlet's hair.
This shell of a mussel is the badge for pilgrims
Bound to places of devotion
Beyond the sea —
In a day, old Fortinbras is defeated; the new Hamlet

Cries into this Fool's ear, and the pine weirs
Sank mysteriously into the North Sea...

Past three, still unable to sleep,
In disbelief I heard all four gates
To the churchyard
Opening and closing simultaneously—
Only a devil wind, undercut with wintry air,
Could visit us with such commotion! In the morning,
I was asked by Gertrude to speak of it...
I feigned madness that winter, not answering her,
And, in April, with the gray eyes of potatoes,

They buried me.

The Open Happens in the Midst of Beings

Martin Heidegger

The coroner said a white picket fence,
Passed in a split second,
Will induce a fit in an epileptic...
It was a yellow Jaguar
With a black steamer trunk
Strapped to the rack. He wet himself,
Straightened against the accelerator,
And entered Smith's barn at 90 mph —

He bit through his tongue was all,
Left one cow senseless
But with a sweeter milk. And
A young sow miscarried like a trout,
Just a plug of mucus and suds at the mouth.

You laughed. His wife
Passed the cake. Down at the dock
Two waiters, clearly in love,
Smoked while speaking
To the rocks and lake.

The trees were frantic.

We walked through the pasture
Along the river, so not to be late.
But stopped at the pin oak
Where you stepped out of your skirt
And into the haze of gnats;
By the time they passed, you were
On your back in the water.
Leaf shadow draped over you
From the waist to the feet...

We were asked not to be late.

At dinner the psychic's assistant
Without permission
Took some straw from your hair.
You blushed. I gave her boss
A look that cost him his concentration.
Still, he told your mother

Her license plate number. I frowned
Through the applause, pushing
Olives around with a spoon.
He then hypnotized our red-haired waitress
And a moth flew out of her mouth.

It brought me back to the pin oak
Where, in the midst of beings
Who were weeping, we laughed and swam
Not quite like the undoubted trout
Who were beside themselves
On the riverbed in a cold white spout...

At Midsummer

for Jeannine

We had been in the tall grass for hours—
Sleep coming on some barrier of bells
Waking you—you stretched, the moon lost
In clouds, the gravestones below us
To the north had moved
West to a hill: the white rounded stones,
All at cruel angles to the ground,
Had been white-and-black heifers resting
Beside the stream with its ledges of quartz marl.

Earlier you had thought the stream
Moved like clear muscle and sinew
With their hooks
In the narrow runners of limestone.
You stretched, your breasts uncovered—
You had hurt your back lifting seed basins
Out in the shed; eased,
Touching me, you think of Kabir, saying:

Worlds are being told like beads.
The day began with the famous airs of a catbird,
A white unstruck music, you were downstairs
Sweeping mouse dirt out of the cupboards.
Now, down in the grass I am awake. I look over
To the north. And say: *It's gone? The gravestones?*
You smile and cross over me like a welcome storm.

Parish

for my parents

I.

God only knows what he'd been doing. Painting or sewing?
All I can say is that from my window
In the old yellow-and-black parsonage
I had been looking across falling snow
To the brick mortuary on the other side of the road.
It had one lamp burning; the mortician
Had thrown off his white gown, washed
His hands above the forearms, was exhausted,
And sat down. The water still running.

II.

I had a little friend once
Who fixed her own dolls: the walleyed, the lame,
And the gutted. She lived in a small town like this one.
She grew up to be odd.
All day I'd waited for a visitor
Who wasn't coming, all highways
Now closed by bad weather.

III.

He'd left the water running cold over porcelain.
He'd thrown down his gown. Looked out at the road.
Hypnotized by the snow and running water,
He gazed off to the body of hills.

IV.

The wind grew for some hours, then it was dawn.
The storm over. I could see footprints
That had shallowed with the drifting snow, that had
Come to our door in the dark—

Perhaps some transient
Looking for an early breakfast after a night
Of journeying and enchantment. I smelled
Dahlias—thoughts of Saint Jerome's lion
            Carrying a burden of wood in for the stove.
            I glanced
            To the footprints,
            Which had circled, waited; circled some more,
            And left our door, leaping the fence

            Or passing through it, all signs
            Of them vanishing into the hills.

Revelations

circa 1948

I.

I made no sound, at all, like the wintering
Of the paper wasp, or milch cattle
In fog,
Or the mud-caked winesaps in the cellar.
I just watched the neighbor
Up in the ladder with his torch.
The wooly nests of the tent caterpillars
Swelled as he sent them off with fire.
All that morning he poured Clorox
Down the anthill under the linden.
I read about children gone mad
With the shelling in Jerusalem.

It was two nights before
Charles Cobb stood outside his barn
And saw beyond the potatoes
A triangle of blue lights
Revolve above his firepond. The newspaper
Said it was *other beings*, and it spoke
Of war in the Holy Land. That night
The neighbor climbed into the elm again
With a torch. An hour passed,
Then he grabbed at his heart! He was there
Until morning in the big gnarled
Crotch of the tree. I slept in the window

Seeing in my dream the neighbor
Twenty years earlier, in a January thaw,
The flash point of his rifle in the pines,
Deer running out onto the pond, the ice
Breaking under them, just antlers

Thrashing above water like the dark bare
Branches of sumac that are there now.
A span of mules
Dragged the frozen deer up the winter road.

   II.

Out of my mother's sleep I heard those light
Watery ovations in the spring onions.
I woke to watch the black ant
Milk the happy aphid right on the rose.
I listened to the hoarse *chack-chack*
Of the partridge working like the adze blade
In the woods. At dusk I looked up
At the hill, the caterpillars were spewing
Their gauze boxes again in the elm.
The neighbor's son was out to get them.

A whole year
The ladder had lain there on the ground.
The neighbor's boy walked it up
Into the tree, dipped his torch of rags
Into gasoline, and lit them. On the night breeze
A sleeve of fire drifted down behind him
And splattered on the lawn where the weight
Of the ladder's drowse had left its image
As dead grass which began to burn
Missing, like the ladder itself,
A high rung.
     I watched. And made no sound...

Elegy for Wright & Hugo

Saint Jerome lived with a community
Of souls in a stone house.
He had a donkey and a young lion.
Winter evenings the brown donkey
Went out for wood, the proud lion
Always his faithful companion.

One night passing merchants seized
The donkey. The lion
Returned to the house
And was accused by Jerome
Of having eaten his friend!
The punishment was merciful — the lion
Assumed the donkey's burden
And went alone each winter evening
Across the fields
For firewood. The lion missed
The donkey, but he never
Felt wronged or misunderstood.

Years passed. And then
The merchants, with troubled conscience,
Detailing their shame, returned the donkey
To Saint Jerome.
The donkey and the lion
Resumed happily their winter schedules.
Everyone was forgiven. This is where
The story usually ends.

But months passed
And the lion, who missed his new usefulness,
Changed, became jealous, and snapped —

He ate the donkey under the stars
Among the cold alders.

He returned to the stone house
With a load of wood on his back.
Saint Jerome, not to be confused by experience,
Announced to the community
That the donkey was again lost,
That the lion had returned
With firewood, that the lion was bloody,
No doubt from combat, no doubt having attacked
The cruel merchants who had once again
Stolen his companion. But Jerome knew—
From then on the downcast lion
Was excused from all work, was left
To age by the fire.

Jerome, dressed in sack,
Went out each night
Barefoot across the blue snow
And returned with branches
Tied to his back.

He was a saint. It was like that...

New England, Springtime

Emerson thought the bride had one eye
Boring into the dark cellar. You stand
In the dry tub shaking powder over your shoulders.
The neighborhood is busy.

It is like anxiety: housepainters dressed in white,
Two hold a ladder while the third climbs;
Drenched in sunlight they are blind travelers
In a vertical landscape of cut ivory.

On my mother's veranda the addled missionary drinks tea.
She says
That in India if a child is bitten
By a cobra, the villagers leave at the site
A saucer of milk and hibiscus flowers. She says
That in India there is fur on a struck bell
Like fur on a bee. A toad eats a fly.
A toad sleeps. Out in the cistern

There is the great gone stomach of algae.

While the missionary speaks, we drag
An open sheet of newspaper behind us, we rise
And then kneel, with a spade we are burying
The heads of sunfish in the roots of rosebushes.
It will feed the flowers. Emerson thought
His bride
Had her one eye on the cool hams in the cellar.

Later, on a walk, we stand on a train trestle
And hold each other:
We are lost watching the hot track reach back

Under the flowering trees, the track
Has white pollen on it to the vanishing point.
It is unsustainable in the long day,

Cattle cars rattling by at sunset.

The Elegy for Integral Domains

You watched the slender narcissus wilt
In the vase below the pulpit.
You could never explain how the brain
Was packed with light, or that memory of a circus:
White undigested bone in tiger filth. The fear
Suddenly let go of you while you watched
The rich jeweler in the pew
Across the aisle. His hair fell down
That side of his face where the eyepiece stayed —
You wondered about skin wrinkled
From looking at jewels,
And then the fear left you with the wind
Over the pond, with the swelling
Of the church organ. There was the sweet smell
Of boiled corn in a cold night kitchen. The risible
Life of a spider living in a dry cracked flute,
And fog, you wrote, in the straw of the universe.

We can never be the undoubted stone.
Dice and mathematics. Music and the storm.
You loved the reticence of something
Heard first from the oboe. Some secret
Not heard from the solo instrument. And
Then runs of it in the orchestra. You heard of Schumann
In the asylum at Endenich near Bonn,
The white Schumann sprawled on the bed,
The attendant flicking at the tube to the enema bag.

You loved your wife, but the undoubted stone
Has no life in it. The diamondback pattern
On the cloth of the hose to the vacuum cleaner
Ran in and out of time, ran
From your mouth to the exhaust of the Plymouth.

Your brother gave me your journal, asking me
To write this. It made a hag of me in a night.
You loved life.
There is no way someone can make himself ready

To say this: a man dragging
A Christmas tree out of the woods found a body.

Arkhangel'sk

The yellow goat in winter sunlight
Is eating a birch canoe.
The carrot fields are black.
Snow is falling like sawdust. Joseph Stalin

And his barber are in fine spirits
This morning. It is the first day of Lent.
They are laughing about a prisoner
Who in three nights of questioning
Confessed repeatedly
To having painted over
A fresh cocoon on a garden fence.

The prisoner
Is dying on a narrow canvas cot.
He has dragged his last shoe of coal
Through the camp. He did not die of the cold.
He died of typhus: crying first

For his sister, then for their yellow goat
Who ate asters,
And finally for the lake cottage —
Bullets rippling like moles under the plaster.

Nine Black Poppies for Chac

I.

The junta was jubilant around the mortised fountain.
A solemn procession of century plants going to the bridge.
A dead chauffeur in the ditch.
You thought
You watched a quetzal bird fly from the bursting tin
Of gasoline. Nine enemies of the junta
Are sprawling in the back of an open Mercedes.
You threw your last two paintings into the sea. Looked
For snow on the mountain.
You washed your legs and breasts in a jagged fragment
Of mirror glass. And wrote, *Except for the groin,*
My body is seamless. I've changed my mind about God again.

II.

Near the shack your Winchester kicks once —
In your line of vision the lifting hawk did not drop
For it had eclipsed briefly a crow, your lead passed
Through its black stomach:
                              the hawk banks to the left,
Free-falls, tucked
For one complete revolution, then wielding suddenly
Onto the immaculate screw of a rising thermal,
It rose a degree or two on the horizon and made
Its quick diagonal hit at the neck of the dead crow.
It took only a moment. You fed the chickens corn, and
Threw the Winchester into the ocean.
The dead colonel in the Mercedes wore his winter coat
Like a cape, arms absent from the sleeves. For this
You dislike him even more. The newspaper talked
About the contents of his mistress's stomach. The colonel
Had made a sautéed abalone.

Abalone, like inkfish,
Needs prodigious pounding with a pine mallet.
The red foot of this shellfish is butchered
Like a steak. When the fat reaches the point of fragrance
Cook two minutes to each side.
>   *Oh yes, parsley*
>   *to clean the palate first.*
You hoped you had watched a quetzal bird flit
In and out, alongside the limousine,
Below the green stand of cane...
>   *and a cavity*
>   *was cut deep into the colonel's loins;*
>   *it was*
>   *irrigating pink in the eternal spring rains.*

The Widow of the Beast of Ingolstadt

A fork in the garden, the widow digging
Behind her elms
Lives like a mouse with the esteem of a few flowers.

She watches at dusk
While the indigo bunting, out of its cage,
Walks through a plague of snails
That is still smoldering. The gardener
Killed them with gasoline and a long trench, it was
Lye the last time. She thought

Of Pastor Bonhoeffer, who plotted
Against Hitler, and the other prisoners
In the canvas truck
That burned wood, the *chuff-chuff*
Of steam up the late winter road
From Buchenwald to Flossenbürg—all of
Them hanged in the morning, in the background
The white outbursts of an acetylene torch
Up in the eaves of the S.S. barracks...

The widow last night was reading
The third testament, just a row of birches
Swaying in the breeze, and she felt aged—

Then, in all of a moment, she knew
Her husband's watch had just stopped in his grave.

Meister Eckhart

All day the snow festered
In the balsams

And then the sun set...
His great providence

Increased with furs, he shook
And vomited. He gnawed

Again at a cold wing
Of pheasant.

Outside the window, some
Poor farmers

Struggled in the yard:
A hog that died earlier

In the thaw of afternoon
Would not be subtracted

From the frozen mud
Through which it had plowed.

The air
Was ecstatic with cold.

The bull of John xxii, dated
January 7, 1327, speaks

Of him as being, this night,
Dead. It says

He first renounced his heresies,
And then was lifted...

Eckhart, a mystic,
Had thought

That a stone to the extent
That it is being

Is greater than God, for
Being could not be subtracted

From it. That was his.
He taught that being aware

Of what God is not, we still
Are ignorant of what God is...

And creatures of themselves,
He said,

Are pure nothings.
Before the gathered Franciscans,

Before the Inquisition, he spoke
Of a love that seizes us —

While he spoke
The hemorrhage rose to his mouth —

Before the assembly
He concluded his defense, observing

That the last light
Was leaving their proceedings...

He choked back the blood, saying
That is enough for the present.

And he meant it.

Dream

It was the Sung Dynasty.
They wore pleated red jackets. Virtually children —
I saw that she had concealed
In her hand a quartz blade and something
Like the dark leaves of hepatica.
There had been torrential rains
For three days. The young couple had walked
All morning to reach a waterfall and its pool;
They now knelt before each other
In an ester mist rising from pitcher plants.

It was spring and the boy's father
Would tomorrow flee with his family inland
To escape invading Tartars.
The spider who lived behind the mirror brought
Good luck, his father had said; it died
The day the rains began. The rains had weakened
Cliffs of decayed limestone that were miles
Above where the couple had knelt
Beside a waterfall to kiss. I said she opened
Her hand, she held a tiny quartz knife
And mossy stonecrop. He nodded to her,
And the distant limestone cliffs with a hillside
Of firs slid down into the river, choking it.

The stonecrop fell to her lap. The river slowed,
And then,
The waterfall stopped.

The Diamond Persona

for L.

I dreamt Tolstoi was mad and running away
By train to the north.
My wife and brothers
Built for me a forty-foot tower
With a platform of reeds where like Saint Simeon
I either sat or stood
In all weather for more than six years.

The tower consisted of four rooted trees
Drawn in at their waists
By a diamond-shaped tourniquet of hemp,
The ropes went out in all directions at once
Like a desperate prayer
That brings emptiness and trembling and then
A centering peace.

Pails brought my meals and took away my waste.
It was rumored the Czar would visit.
By the first summer
The campfires stretched out for miles
At my feet. Ladders were hung from my tower
And peasants brought me children
To be healed; aristocrats and scholars
Asked in detail about my visions. By the second winter
I stopped all but the ritual meal of bread and cheese.
I bled like sleeves from a body. Over the years
The people forgot me.

Early in the last spring I knew
I was dying. I gave instructions to my acolytes
And by twilight my platform was soaked
In kerosene, the fire was set,

And with one pass of a large French blade
A strongman from Mongolia cut
The fraying ends of the diamond tourniquet — burning
I flew into the heavens.

My body was found in a near field
And I was buried there.
My only regret is that our beloved mother
Abandoned us as children for literature,
Which gave us ideals, only soon afterward
To abandon literature for religion,
Only *then* deciding
That everything was meaningless

Except the life of her youngest son, who, in devotion
To his mother, would fly and burn like the sun
Above some fanciful future spring planting.

La Pampa

The dead truck sits in the shimmering wheat.
The vegetables on the sill were meant to go
To seed. Looking past them there is a tomb.
Beyond the tomb, in the heat, two boys
Enter a grove they were told not to: in the branches
Is the drying skin of a black bull
Slaughtered that noon, the boy's father
Sits on the ground in the dripping shadow of the skin.
He is eating plums. Last night, their newborn sister

Slept beside the paraffin stove, their mother
Had left some of her milk in a cup
In the icebox, it was blue, sticky,
And too sweet, they thought. Their grandfather
In fever spoke of the judges of the dead,
Of the words of necessity:
>   *A young librarian*
> *Went straight in the chair, a tooth lost*
> *In her upper lip.* They were so silent
While they knelt there in the grove — they felt
It was just their luck that at the moment
Their father stood to dust himself off
The younger brother was seized, it seemed, by hiccups.
The next winter he fell into the well. Past midnight
The older brother remembers while the sergeant
Tortures the young librarian
In white pajamas and turquoise slippers.

The Funeral

It felt like the zero in brook ice.
She was my youngest aunt; the summer before
We had stood naked
While she stiffened and giggled, letting the minnows
Nibble at her toes. I was almost four—
That evening she took me
To the springhouse where on the scoured planks
There were rows of butter in small bricks, a mold
Like ermine on the cheese,
And cut onions to rinse the air
Of the black, sickly-sweet meats of rotting pecans.

She said butter was colored with marigolds
Plucked down by the marsh
With its tall grass and miner's-candles.
We once carried the offal's pail beyond the barn
To where the fox could be caught in meditation.
Her bed linen smelled of camphor. We went

In late March for her burial. I heard the men talk.
I saw the minnows nibble at her toe.
And Uncle Peter, in a low voice, said
The cancer ate her like horse piss eats deep snow.

Sanctuary

My sister got me the script. I couldn't
Believe it. To work for Charles Barzon.
He was doing a film of *Thérèse Raquin*.
Zola's novel. The wife is in love
With her sickly husband's best friend;
They are on an outing—an accident is staged
On the river. They drown
The husband. The river takes him.
Then begin
The visits to the Paris morgue:
Each day from a balcony
They look down at a flat, turning wheel;
Eight naked corpses, unclaimed,
Revolving on a copper-and-oak bed.
A fine mist
Freshening the bodies. I was
To be one of them. I almost said no.

But Barzon's a genius. He took us aside,
One at a time. He gave us
Secret lives, even though we were the dead.
I was Pauline,
A sculptor's model of the period.
I would have to shave my groin,
Armpits, and legs.
Hairless, Pauline was a strange euphemism.
What is the scripture,
The putting on of nakedness?

"You'll be like marble," Barzon said.

I felt a little sick
With the slow revolutions and lights.

The cold mist raised my nipples.
My hair was ratted and too tight.
Between takes, we shared from boredom
Our secret lives:
To my right was a plowman, kicked
In the chest by a horse. He staggered,
Barzon had told him, out of the field
Into the millrace.
To my left, a thief who had been knifed
In a Paris street. We were spread-eagled,
Cold, and hungry. I looked over to the thief
Who was, to my surprise, uncircumcised...
I said, "Verily, this day you will be
With me in Paradise." For a moment the dead
In their places writhed—
Barzon was so upset saliva flew from his lips.

The dream occurred that night. And every
Night since.
Three weeks now, the same dream:
One of the carpenters from the set
Is on a high beam way above us.
I don't know how I see him past the lights.
But there he is, his pants unzipped.
I scream. Barzon looks up from a camera
And says, "Get that son of a bitch."
The workman slips
Just as a floodlight touches him.
Before he hits the floor, I'm awake.
The first thing I realize
Is that I'm not a corpse, not dead,
Then, in horror,
I see I am still naked and Thérèse Raquin's
Drowned husband
Is sitting accusingly at the foot of my bed.

The Duchesse's Red Shoes

after Proust

I.

Swann has visited the Duc and Duchesse de Guermantes,

And now he is walking his horse the first kilometer
Through the woods down to the road. It is his shortcut.
The two roads entering the Guermantes estates
First circle back before returning to the front gates
As if to ask

Whether or not to arrive correctly at eight. One autumn day
Swann's drunken coachman, finding the north road
To the estates, fell asleep and the horses
Coming to the loop, not to be delayed,
Not wanting to saunter back through the gardens before
Making the gate, simply raised their heads, snorted
In the cold air, and with little difficulty

Plowed through the Duchesse's bed of champagne-marigolds;
White mud plastered their legs as they stopped before
An astonished black servant-in-livery.
And Swann with his laughter woke his coachman.
The coachman promising to shoot himself in the head
That very evening, only after saying good-bye
To his children.

Swann kissed the man's cheek and asked him to see that
The horses got sugar with their feed.

II. THE VISIT

The Duc and Duchesse de Guermantes loved Swann. Their friend
Was always welcomed by them personally, even in the morning.

And now Swann is walking his sorrel horse back the first
Kilometer through dripping poplars—
Earlier in the day in a poor district of Paris
Swann had sat before a doctor who was eating
A potato with dried beef.
It was not even a matter of months! Days, perhaps, the doctor
Added, as he threw the potato peel out the window.

Swann said, "Oh, I see, then I'll be leaving you, doctor."
The doctor continued eating. Swann thought him refreshingly
Decent. The doctor looked up from his plate only after Swann
Had put a door between them. The doctor then reached
Into his shirt pocket for three fat radishes that
He had thought better of eating in front of this poor soul
Who was soon to be ashes in blue pottery that sits
In a gold plate.

     III.

Swann had gone to the estate that afternoon to tell his
Friends he was dying. His friends were leaving
For a party.

"What's that you say?" cried the Duchesse, stopping for
A moment on the way to the carriage. She was
Saying to herself, "He is dying?" The Duc, now,
Insisting they will be late for the party. Getting into
The carriage, her skirts raised, she heard her husband cry:

Oriane, what have you been thinking of! You've kept on
Your black shoes. Where are your red shoes, Oriane? He was
Rushing her back into the house. The Duchesse saying, "But
Dear, now we will be late!" The Duc explains that proper
Shoes are more important than the hour of the day. Looking

Back, the Duc says to Swann, "I'm dying of hunger!"
Swann says that the black shoes didn't offend his taste.

The Duc replies, "Listen, all doctors are asses. You are
As strong as Pont Neuf. Now, Oriane, please hurry." Swann
Wonders if this was an expression of love, or courage?

Swann pauses in the woods to watch his friends' speeding
Carriage make that loop through the gardens—
The carriage tips this and that way. Suddenly from
The Duchesse's window a pair of black slippers waves a
Farewell. Swann turns away.

IV. THE DUCHESSE AFTER THE BURIAL

Poor Swann, death, you know, is shy. Death says
That no one can take a bath for you.
And Swann, the Bishop would hate me for this,
But death says no one else can die for you.
Not on crossed sticks even with Romans tossing bones
Below you. Not in any circumstance. Oh, Swann,

Your horses went wild again—in the cemetery!
I thought the graves were opening. The Duc said as
We were leaving you, that day of the red shoes, "No one
Can eat, sleep, or make love for another."
I said, "Your mother when you were inside her ate for another.
A man with a worm eats for another. And often, dear,
A woman makes love for another who is her lover, customer,
Or husband."

Swann, your horses soiled the Bishop's gown
And destroyed the six fern-pots
Of Charlemagne's Cross, the Iron Stair of Violets
Looked more like a broken orchard ladder afterward,
And your hearse, missing its forewheel, stopped finally
In one of those shallow ornamental ponds.
There were dropped prayer books all over the ground.
Your horses, their work done, drank deeply from the pond.

Your wonderful, drunken coachman with a black bottle
Of beer raised above him
Delivered a strange and genuine eulogy, then falling
Backward into the water in which your horses

Were peacefully urinating. I insisted we leave then.
The Duc said that you had not yet
Been placed in the ground. I said you had returned
To that element from which so much life has sprung—

The chaos of a small pond.

Danse Macabre

The broken oarshaft was stuck in the hill
In the middle of chicory,
Puke-flowers, the farmers called them, sturdy
Little evangels that the white deer drift through…

Nobody on the hill before
Had heard of a horse
Breaking its leg in a rowboat. But the mare
Leapt the fence, passed
The tar-paper henhouse,
And then crumpled at the shore.

It was April and bees were floating
In the cold evening barn; from the loft
We heard them shoot the poor horse.
We tasted gunpowder and looked
While your cousin, the sick
Little bastard, giggled and got
So excited he started to dance
Like the slow sweeping passes
Of a drawing compass—

Its cruel nail to its true pencil.

New England, Autumn

Our daughter dreamt of magnolias—
That one mammal among flowers.

You dreamt of bluets
And the hearts of celery. The cat
Had dreamt of his old sock
And the black
Beetle scratching inside the matchbox.

We burned the toast.

The whole house peppered with the cold.
I missed the shadowy hardpan of the desert floor
With the smoke trees and paloverde.
You both asked about my dream.

It was evening.
My dead grandmother was in the yard
That sloped down to the pond:
She'd carefully placed a linen tablecloth
Over the clotheshorse for drying...

I watched a mosquito,
Which rose from the back of my hand
Heavy with blood, vanish
Into the caption of a saw toothed mouth—
The old pike
Striking from under the lily pads.

In a matter of seconds that blood had traveled
From my heart
To the very bottom of the chilled pond.

I woke with a start as if we had set an alarm.

Through a Glass Darkly

after Ingmar Bergman

They are out bathing in the sea at night
With long white legs and arms, the fallen bones
Of the shoulders like heavy tack in the barn
That their ungoverned breasts swing from,
A silhouette of pine at the groin, ink
There and in the eyes,
The wet rope of hair down the back,
The buttocks coarse with the cold air
Like sack. They are my young cousins — insomniacs

Who have just come
From making love to their husbands.

With sand they first washed the seed
From their thighs. I sat on the rocks
And bit
Into the stiff salted skin of fish.

I want them to be this happy.

As children hiding behind the lilacs
We huffed together over the tiny iron file,
When we were done there was one brass tooth
Left on the spool of my mother's music box.
It wasn't much of a song but I taught it

To God while cowering behind the cold radiator
In the long hall of the hospital.
My dead mother was also troubled.
The novel of her death

Went to the publishers the day after she died.
My father's books are sold in six languages.

He hates this island.

My husband is a doctor; he has a nightmare
In which a neon light flashes
A caduceus and then a dollar sign.

He would leave Sweden. He still might.
My cousins have stepped out of the sea.

Looking exhausted
And heavy in their hooded robes,
The sand slowing them, they walk
Across to me like the Franciscans
Who escort us to and from shock therapy…

The Trolley from Xochimilco

for Aimee

I.

The late-afternoon rain stopped. The electric trolley
Did not. You looked up
From your pencil sketch of a bird's nest
Upset on the skull of a forgotten doge. The trolley

Struck the wooden bus at the center bench, the bus
Stretched forever and then burst —
The Virgin of Guadalupe scattering with the pigeons.
A block away people had fallen in waves
Before the splintering wood. It was not raining
Anywhere in Mexico City. The Red Cross ambulance

Was coming. The collision
Took your dress:
A rail passed through your stomach,
They drew it out of you on the street, your scream
Opened rain clouds over the cathedral and shops.

A baker passed
With his intestines gathered in his arms. A painter's
Little packet of gold dust, mixed with your blood,
Made your body shocking to passersby
Who felt they had seen enough.

You were eighteen and had proclaimed to friends
Over sherbet that you would
Have the baby of Diego Rivera. That night
Coarse with morphine you told the doctors

You lost your virginity at the corner
Of Cuahutemotzin and 5 de Mayo. They laughed,

You screamed like a horse...

  II.

Death is the favorite doll of little girls. I saw
Her tonight standing on a heap of coal in Detroit.
I hate the gringo dream of being important. Their
Little cocktails honoring this and that *gran caca...*

But they buy Diego's paintings. I want a banquet
Of pulque and squash blossoms.
I have painted my long skirt, maroon and green,
And put it on a powder-blue hanger in Manhattan.

Kiss the little girl. I will always paint
For her with my eyes. A kiss
Is like a dress falling off a tall building.
I miss the monkey and the fence of organ cactus—

I will write more before we take the boat.
Sleep, your Frida will not cut Diego's throat.

  III.

It is better to go, to go.
FRIDA KAHLO

It was an electric trolley from the floating gardens.
The first Indians to discover them
Were searching for food,
Were drugged by the scent of orchids, white mint,
And islands of gentian—when they woke
They found everything moved...

To the groin you were prepared with tinctures
For the operation: the ether became

Your favorite cartoon of a log being sawed.
Returned to the house,
In silence, you took a leg from each
Of the dolls, telling the large pail-baby, Diego,
Who still loved you, that it was a cruel revenue
Worthy of this government

That wore one white shoe. A great woman, and trouble!
They sent you flowers.
The flowers moved...

It was a reluctant telegraph of women, at dawn,
Passing from an upper bedroom, to the parlor,
To the foyer, to his man,
The old chauffeur
On the lawn with a handful of dead snails—
He crossed over to Diego, saying:
Miss Frida is no longer with us! A bird
Flew from the palms. It was a problem. For you
Had made him understand: our bodies

Are long. You touch me.
Our hands plunged in oranges:
You breathe, a tambourine,
My back arched, lifting off the sheets,
You are kissing my breasts, you are kissing

The plaster rosettes of the ceiling.

The Huts at Esquimaux

for Dave Smith

Our clothes are still wet from wading
The Chickamauga last evening.
There is heavy frost. We have
Walked on the dead all night.
Now in the firelight
We are exchanging shells and grapeshot.

I can still hear our loud huzzah
When late in the day
The enemy fell into full retreat
Along the pine ridge to the east...

We chased them until we were weary.
Each night this week
There's been something
To keep me from sleep. Just an hour ago
I saw

A dead sharpshooter sitting
Against a rock with a scallop
Of biscuit still lodged in his mouth.
He wore one silk sock.

Snediker has returned from Chattanooga
With five thousand convalescents
For the left wing of their musketry.

We have roasted a deer
With a molasses sauce and pepper.
Magrill and Zandt have returned
From horse hunting with a sack of sugar.

By morning we will have buried our dead
And fed the prisoners: Joe Cotton

Will hang all seven of them in one tree
When he sees they're done
Licking their fingers...

I shot a Rebel yesterday
In high water just for cursing me.
Just six months ago
For that alone it would have meant
Three days in stockade.

We can see now that cannonading
Has set the hillside on fire.
The wounded Grays
Will be burned
Beyond their Christian names...

Joe Cotton says he'd ask God
For rain, but he's got no tent
And river water
Has chilled him straight through

To the very quick of his being.

Oration: Half-Moon in Vermont

A horse is shivering flies off its ribs, grazing
Through the stench of a sodden leachfield.

On the broken stairs of a trailer
A laughing fat girl in a T-shirt is pumping
Milk from her swollen breasts, cats
Lapping at the trails. There's a sheen of rhubarb
On her dead fingernail. It's a humid morning.

Tonight, with the moon washing some stars away,
She'll go searching for an old bicycle in the shed;
She'll find his father's treasures:
Jars full of bent nails, a lacquered bass,
And the scythe with spiders
Nesting in the emptiness of the blade
And in the bow of its pine shaft.
Milling junk in the dark,

She'll forget the bicycle, her getaway,
And rescue
A color photograph of an old matinee idol.
Leaving the shed, she'll startle

An owl out on the marsh. By November
It will be nailed through the breast to the barn.

In a year the owl will go on a shelf in the shed
Where in thirty years there will be a music box
Containing a lock of hair, her rosaries,
Her birth certificate,

And an impossibly sheer, salmon-pink scarf. What
I want to know of my government is

Doesn't poverty just fucking break your heart?

An Annual of the Dark Physics

The Baltic Sea froze in 1307. Birds flew north
From the Mediterranean in early January.
There were meteor storms throughout Europe.

On the first day of Lent
Two children took their own lives:
Their bodies
Were sewn into goatskins
And were dragged by the hangman's horse
The three miles down to the sea.
They were given a simple grave in the sand.

The following Sunday, Meister Eckhart
Shouted that a secret word
Had been spoken to him. He preached

That Mary Magdalene
Sought a dead man in the tomb
But, in her confusion, found
Only two angels laughing...

This was a consequence of her purity

And her all too human grief.
The Baltic Sea
Also froze in 1303 —
Nothing happened that was worthy of poetry.

The Lion Grotto

Nothing odd.

The pink adobe wall holds the shadows
Of the children
Who have shucked oysters
Onto a fresh bed of shaved ice.
Behind them, out of nowhere,
Is the long straw-colored
Plumb line with its brass bob.

From the kitchen comes the first smell
Of just the gas burner being lit,
The struck match tossed into the shallow sink.

Lizards run the arbor wall.
The house settled during the war
And the faults were paved
With black pitch with clear bubbles
In it like saliva.

The delphiniums of the courtyard, the daffodils,
And witchgrass are gone. Last summer
From the hill they watched the desert
And the switchbacked roads
But their father did not come home.

The bodies of seven men
Are still somewhere in the old south shaft
Of the copper mine.
They were pumping water bitter as lime.

The children listen for the mountain cats
At night. The oldest boy with a peso

On a string around his neck
Stares at a photograph in which

A half-frozen buffalo eats
Bunchgrass beside a hot spring, the snow
Drifting with the vapors, a geyser climbing
Into the dark winter sky. Two seasons
With a grazing margin of compromise.
He'll ask again why things die.

The Train

Accident could be a god to little boys.

The way they hurt their necks
To look through glass down to the twisted
Wreckage in the gorge. The conductor
Telling the ladies from Jamaica
We are one stop from the border. The older
Of the two is shocked by a sudden pasture
Beside the lake, icehouses
Left there for the summer—she says, "Oh, Chloe,
Look at the shanties; to think
There is such poverty in Maine." She begins
To finger the pearls sewn into the shoulder
Of her dress; the diamond she's wearing
Has the fire of fat in it. And then
A tunnel, and then more birches with the lake again.

You smile at me and look across
To the girl in black stockings who is asleep,
Her lips
Moving, her skirt rising with the jumping train.
You straighten your blouse. Sharing
A thermos of coffee, we have said twice
That we'll be late for the station. Beyond the window
The day lilies are a smudged crayon.

Who is drowning in the lake? Whose father
Is falling on the stairs? Which of us
Racing north will be truly late? We are
All annoyed, stepping out into the rain.
The city that we raced for, racing for its own sake.
The girl in black stockings is waking on the corner.

She has ruined the hard parallelism of the rain.
She said her brother died in the jungle last week.
We said, with intonation, what a shame.

Lamentations

The scrubwoman for the old bank and jailhouse,
Her face reddening

Over supper on a steamy night,
Is thinking of the village spillway being

Answered by a dry clucking over mud, *she is*
Touching the burs on the tongue of the azalea...

Exhaustion puts knotted rags in the neck
And shoulders:

As a girl, in Poland, she watched her husband
Be dragged through the shade of five pines

To the execution wall. A year earlier
She had watched him bathe

In the bronze tub the landlord had put
Out in the field as a trough for horses.

She picked him from among the men
Smoking pipes after haying, *she rolled*

Over on her stomach
To study the blue cornflower; she shyly
Rained on the wildflowers, a hot urine...
They laughed, and never knew her brother

Was taken by train to Hamburg, was infected
With tuberculosis, was

In the last days of the war
Stripped along with six other children

And hanged in the boiler room of a post office.
What she has understood

Is there are only
Two speeches the naked make well:

One is of welcome; the other, farewell.

Old Night and Sleep

for my grandfather

A cold rain falls through empty nests, a cold rain
Falls over the canvas
Of some big beast with four stomachs
Who eats beneath a white tree
In which only a dozen dry pods are left...

Some new sense of days being counted.

Ars Poetica

It is almost polio season. The girls

From the cigarette factories in Massachusetts
Are still visiting the northern beaches.
At midnight, the milky rubbers
In the breakers are like a familiar invasion

Of sea life.
Sitting on the rocks we watch a runner:
Weight shifted, some *tick, tick,*
Almost of intelligence —
The bone catching of balance...

From behind, a red-haired girl appears —
Missing a thumb on her left hand,
Breathless, she asks for a light:
A crumpled pack of Lucky Strikes
At the top of a nylon stocking;
The other leg bare, her abdomen
And breasts plastered with white sand.
Drunk, she says, "He just swam out
Past the jetty — that was twenty minutes
Ago. You think I give a damn?"

We lit the cigarette for her. Her hands
Shaking.

No moon, it took an hour
To find all her clothing,
Dropped as they ran
Down the rock shelf through dunes...

He hadn't drowned. He swam around the jetty,
Crawled to the grasses and over the granite shelf.
Gathering his clothes, he left
Her there as a joke.

Her hair was colored
That second chaste coat of red on the pomegranate.
We were eating sandwiches on the rocks.
She frightened my mother and me. My little
Sister just thought she was funny.
In thirty years I have dreamt of her twice, once
With fear and once without. I've written
This for her, and because

Twice is too often
Considering how beautiful she was.

Baptismal

The lightning inside the black cloud put slabs
Of amethyst in the sky. We took the wine
And went inside the old garden house for shelter.
Anne had gone to a cremation that Friday. She said
That in the heat
All the rope in the corpse shortens and dries,
The body slowly rises to a sitting position,
And in the updraft of the furnace
The hair stands on end. Then, the hair burns, she said.

Bill smiled, saying, "That's a lie, Anne." When I was nine,
Anne responded, we stood over
The old Water Street cemetery. The grass
Wasn't cut and it had been a wet spring
Followed by a long dry summer.
We threw in three matches. Beth, in a simple print dress,
With the wind rising, wet herself and
Took down her panties tossing them into the fire.
The rows of soapstone crosses
Wilted in the flames. Above it all stood
Some smoke-blackened statuary:
A bronze eagle wrestling with a marble snake
And to the north, large female angels
With breasts and extended wings, their attention
Was on the snake
And in the shimmering heat they began
To walk over the fire like a lake.

Poem

A mule kicked out in the trees. An early
Snow was falling,
The girl walked across the field
With a hairless doll—she dragged
It by the green corduroy of its sleeve
And with her hands
Buried it beside the firepond.

The doll was large enough to make a mound
Which she patted down a dozen times.
Then she walked back alone.
The weak winter sun
Sat on the horizon like a lacquered mustard seed.

She never noticed me
Beside the road drinking tea from a thermos.
The noisy engine cooling.
Did you ever want to give someone

All your money? We drove past midnight, ate,
And drove some more—unable to sleep in Missouri.

Trakl

for Paul & Doug

In reality the barn wasn't clean, ninety men
Charged to you:
The burns, missing teeth, and dark jawbone
Of gnawed corn, gangrene from ear to elbow—
Even the dying
Returned to consciousness by the ammonia of cows.

You ran out looking beyond your hands
To the ground, above you a wind
In the leaves: looking up you found
Hanged partisans convulsing in all the trees.

Down the road in the garrison hospital,
In a cell for the insane, you were given
Green tea and cocaine...
With the blue snow of four o'clock
Came peace and that evening of memory
With Grete, her touch—in yellow spatterdock
She tied a black ribbon
Around the cock of a sleeping horse.
It was her *vivacious littles* as an admirer
Once put it. *Sister, trough...*

How men talk. I read you first
In an overly heated room,
Sitting in an open window. I left
For a walk in the woods. Coming out
Into a familiar sinkhole, meadow
Now snow, deer ran over the crust—
Hundreds of them. I thought of my two uncles,

Their war, the youngest dead at Luzon,
The other, in shock,
At his barracks in California: Christmas evening
He looked up from the parade grounds and saw
An old Japanese prisoner
With arms raised, from the hands came
A pigeon. The bird climbed, climbed
Slowly and then dissolved

Like smoke from some lonely howitzer
Blossoming out over the bubbling bone pits of lye, over
The large sunken eyes of horticulture.

Jeremiad

After a night of opium and alcohol, Edgar Poe
Walks out of a laundry into the harsh sunlight
Of an affluent Baltimore. From behind, as I see him,
He is not
Of experience, and he is without sin—
He waddles
In the archetype of Charlie Chaplin
And crosses the street to the park
Where yesterday evening yellow swathes of poison
Were dropped on the wind
To kill an unprecedented population
Of ground snails.

Now, Poe is reaching the great lawn of the park
Where swans have been feasting
On the tainted snails. The swans are sick.
Poe, drugged as he is,
Shatters with this vision of vomiting swans. He turns,

And running at him
In a line fifty yards long
Is a pack of stray dogs from everywhere
In Baltimore. They will eat the swans.

Edgar Allan Poe, who stood between them,
Made a judgment—

The hounds of hell were coming for him;
He climbed the statue of a stylish general
On a rearing horse.
He clung to the marble thigh of the stallion.
He watched, in horror, the field below him.
The torn swans were long syllables

Over the ground.
By the time he was able to climb down,
A crowd had formed. He told them, wide-eyed,

He told them what he saw—truth and beauty
Fornicating on the public lawn. Everyone frowned

As they sometimes will in Baltimore.

Groom Falconer

circa 1903

Out walking along the river
I still saw the fever with her children
At supper in the coal light. Snow falling,
I climbed up through the wood
To the asylum to visit with Sister
In the locked ward. But hesitated
And went to the cottage to see the insomniac

Rich child who sits naked at the window:

Last night, in kerosene light, her back
Had a quality of milkglass. She curls
In the chair.
Her knees under her chin, the room black—

The light at the window is all
Moon and snow. She is at it again:
With the nail of the little finger
She has flayed
The thumb of the same hand;
All but the little finger arthritic
With the procedure: the raw thumb

White like a boiled egg
In an upturned palm; the dead skin,
Bits of shell, not polished by hen straw.

Beyond the window there is a sudden
Convulsion of wind in the blue spruce,
Boughs dumping snow. *I imagine*
The brass makeweights that lift the other pan,
Or this past summer, dust and pollen

Rising around oxslaughter. A shudder
Passes through the child, taking
Her attention;

She cuts herself for the first time, a trickle
Of blood at the knuckle of the thumb
Like the single red thread
Through the lace hood and jesses
Of the Medici falcons.
Her concentration broken, the hand
Loosens: *one wing, one stone.*

The sun is seeping over the snow.

She greets me with an acknowledgment
One reserves for a ghost.

Accident

He stood in a green stand of corn
And watched the light of a train
Shrink from the woods and crossing. It became
Absolute: at that last second, just a white dot
On the cab of the stalled truck in which
His daughter, foot off the clutch, fought gears.
The milk of field corn everywhere.
He fell back into the brittle stalks.
In the night an acetylene torch sputtered
Silencing the cicadas up in the cottonwoods.
The red caboose had mowed down corn,
Stopping within ten feet of him.
Two men in overalls with a lantern
Stepped into the field.
They were from Mars. They opened their mouths,
Speaking in the one tongue of the blasted
Cattle cars, the cries
Of the dying animals strewn out behind them.

Fever

for Jeannine

In your sleep you talked.

There are cows standing in white mud.
A bale of hay has fallen out of the sky for them.
The cows are rejoicing,
Standing on their hind legs.
Their rough teats caked
With the white mud.
Their great skulls above the ground fog.

While you talked I bathed you with a sponge
From a basin of ice and alcohol.
I told you that in my childhood,
During the mud season, old boards ran from the house
To the barns and then out into pastureland...

The farmer's wife is walking
On the old boards out to the dancing cows.
She's pissed and wants their milk.
Another bale of hay
Is falling from the sky. It's killed the farmer's wife.
Good enough for her.
The mud is sucking her down. Good-bye.

I said, "You know I love you."

Oh, my god, the farmer's wife is alive.
She's climbing out of the mud
Onto an old board. She looks like a tooth.
Oh, my god, she is a tooth.

I love you too.

Of Politics, & Art

for Allen

Here, on the farthest point of the peninsula
The winter storm
Off the Atlantic shook the schoolhouse.
Mrs. Whitimore, dying
Of tuberculosis, said it would be after dark
Before the snowplow and bus would reach us.

She read to us from Melville.

How in an almost calamitous moment
Of sea hunting
Some men in an open boat suddenly found themselves
At the still and protected center
Of a great herd of whales
Where all the females floated on their sides
While their young nursed there. The cold frightened whalers
Just stared into what they allowed
Was the ecstatic lapidary pond of a nursing cow's
One visible eyeball.
And they were at peace with themselves.

Today I listened to a woman say
That Melville *might*
Be taught in the next decade. Another woman asked, "And why not?"
The first responded, "Because there are
No women in his one novel."

And Mrs. Whitimore was now reading from the Psalms.
Coughing into her handkerchief. Snow above the windows.
There was a blue light on her face, breasts, and arms.
Sometimes a whole civilization can be dying
Peacefully in one young woman, in a small heated room

With thirty children
Rapt, confident and listening to the pure
God-rendering voice of a storm.

The Apocrypha of Jacques Derrida

The ruptured underbelly of a black horse flew overhead.
Bonaparte, is what the matron said to me,
Always condescending; vulgar, slowly separating
The three syllables. And it was the last thing she said.
The engine block struck the tree. Our faces
Making brook ice of the windshield. The vaulting black horse
Now on its side in the dust. I was left
With the road, with the memory of cities burning.
Matron seemed to sleep. My nose bleeding.
I went over to inspect the huge sunflowers
That were beyond the stone wall. The sunflowers
Marched with me in Italy. They were cut down.
There was gasoline everywhere. The attendants
Will come for me. It's back to the island.
I'll study English out in the cool stucco of the shed.
I don't really believe I am the Corsican. But then
Neither did he.
The car was now burning with the tree. The black
Brook ice bursting. The horse got up and left.
A back hoof snared by intestine…

I was once all game leg in a fast sleigh
Passing a half-frozen cook who asked a frozen orderly,
"Is he the snow?"
If only that cook had been my general.
It was that straggling long line that cost us.
If they had moved in a dark swarm, huddled together,
Cloud shadow over the Russian countryside, then
There would have been little trouble, a few men
Out on the fringes dropping to the snow for rest,
But still how
Like a forest they would have been
Moving over the land

Like that gang who came for Macbeth.
I know what you're thinking, that the land pell-mell
Is itself mostly obstacle
And this makes a road. But we were cloud shadow

Moving over snow.

The Death of the Race Car Driver

I have not slept for a week.

It is matchless—this feeling
I have for the dream:

Baled hay burning in the air
With the splintering planks of the barricade.
As I roll
I feel all over me, the silk drapery
Of bony French schoolgirls.

In the last month of the war,
Visiting a friend, I watched
A young nurse
Stare mindlessly past me
While soaping the testicles
Of an unconscious amputee...

At a hundred and eighty miles per hour
There's little vibration in the chassis, a clarity
Like the musical waterglass
Gently tapped, but, here, silent and empty—
Speed and sleep have overlapped. My body,

Sack for eternity.

The Fish

A pale woman is cradling a large red fish
That she's stolen from the hospital kitchen.
She stands in the bright garden
In the cold wind. Black waterlilies
Are gently wrestling her to the gravel's edge.
In the struggle she kisses them
On their mouths. They say, sadly, "Alice, Alice!"
Grasping her red fish
At its banded anus, near the black spines
Of the tail, she knocks them
Unconscious with it. Even in their drowse
The waterlilies trouble Alice.
Her boss, Mr. Calvin, has had surgery—
Is dying now
In the freshly plastered solarium.
She'll be out of work by morning. Her sister
Thinks they are going to lose the house.
Alice was praying for a miracle. They drilled
Holes in his skull. And the red fish
Has fallen in with the waterlilies,
Into the small pond. It shivers, breaks
To the left, leaps into the air, and, then,
Without a thought for Alice,
Swims toward the bottom to sleep in the mud.

Buffalo Clouds over the Maestro Hoon

for my godson

It was a useless thing to do with the morning.

Couples with umbrellas strolled over the lawns
Beside the abyss. The Maestro tossed a fresh bed of straw for
        his friend,
He sipped coffee with chicory,
And, then, attempted to walk over Niagara Falls
On a string while pushing a wheelbarrow
That contained a lion captured in the Congo.
Hoon had copper cleats
Sewn into his silk slippers. He wore the orange gown.
It was the full weight of the lion
That propelled this old man and wheelbarrow
Over the falls…

Of all things this is what
I've chosen to tell you about the world. This,
And the fact that bearded Hoon and his big cat
Faltered, again and again, up in the wind
But were not toppled.

It was a useless thing to do with the morning.
And a glory. The only beauty
In the story is that the lion roared. His voice
Twice lost to the deafening falls; of course,
It was reported that the lion yawned.
The courage of the beast, feigned or not,
Is a lesson in understanding us,
Who are right when we are wrong,
Who see boredom in a toothless lion,
In his *cri de coeur* over a stupefying volume
Of falling water

That sounds like the ovation
Given to Hoon as he stepped
Off his tightrope into the open arms
Of men and women with umbrellas
Still strange to one another while on their honeymoons.

An American Scene

I reach beyond the laboratory brain. The brass
Lamp with its white shade throws the shadow
Of the specimen and the gladiolus in suspension
Against the wall. The gladiolus

Is a fragment of sternum,
Not some iris which would fry in formaldehyde.
The rubber apron hangs on its nail.
There is some color here — the poster
Over the autoclave
Has five red tuna boats
Rising and falling in a black sea.

My mother is marrying again. They stand
In the photograph
Before his honeysuckle hedge in Los Angeles.
I came to Boston because of the earthquakes.
And mother's
Migraines — the light of which is religious.
Mother sincerely believes that Henry James died in 1905
In that Pullman car
Crossing the great alkali desert of Arizona. At least
He wished to is what she believes.

Here all it does is rain. The technician
From C-wing has long brown hair and hazel eyes.
Yesterday, in the middle of the night, for fun
She flattened her bare breasts
Against the window to the lab.
They looked like cow pies whitened by sun.
I stripped and turned off the lamp.
She brought two paper cups
Full of brandy... something the deaf Beethoven wrote

Came over her radio.
I took an old soft paperback
And tucked it under the small of her back.
It was pure lust...
The brain glowed in the dark above us.

Northwind Escarpment

The mirrors in the hall were a strange backwater
Of mercury and leafmold. The walnut table
Was wet with twilight. The standing radio
Had the red static of needles in a pine forest.

Outside the window, beyond the ginkgo,
Two girls with long bare legs were sinking
In the endless mudflats.
Their father in a white suit shook a stick at them.
The girls' laughter seemed a problem for him.

The tide had never withdrawn this far from the house.
Your skirt dropped to your ankles. You unbuttoned
Your blouse. In complete darkness
You walked to the kitchen and washed yourself
From the waist up. You came back
To the piano bench where we shared a cigarette.

While we slept the tide crept in
And the blistered troughs that are rowboats
Banged against one another...

By sunrise we had all died in the war. What's more,
We always knew it was possible.

New Age at Airport Mesa

My husband was hanging wet sheets, almost in disbelief,
When he had his heart attack. It kicked him
In the neck and shoulder; the heavy linen,
Flying backward with him, was sucked darkly
Into his mouth — he was like that Wyoming snowfield
Where the ground above the old cistern collapsed.
I was still grieving when the oleander blossomed.

So Ruth and I rented a cottage for a month. I painted
The stream and poplars. Ruth meditated
And made enough cucumber sandwiches to feed
Us and our dead husbands. She had a vision that third week
Of a naked Navajo giantess eating a peach.
It was so real that the juice of the peach
Ran down her chin and breasts striking the dust
Like a rain of nails. Ruth was delighted with her vision
Until she realized it was meaningless.

Our last afternoon in the cottage she was feeling nauseous
And I was bored
So I visited the canyon for the first time alone. I whistled
A warning to the snakes.
I found a sandstone platform above a young paloverde.
My mind wandered for I don't know how long
Until I realized I had been staring, at some distance,
At two nude women, girls really,
Kneeling before each other and touching themselves:

They began to kiss — they were both blond, it was
More like one woman and a mirror. What they did I wouldn't
Tell you. But toward the end I could even hear them.
As I listened to their cries rising above the desert,

I began to cry with them. The hot wind
Dried my tears. It dried their mouths, their whole bodies...

Later when I told Ruth she amazingly approved
And announced it was a vision. I agreed
So she would stop talking... I smiled.
Sat on the couch.
I told her I was done feeling sorry for myself.

Shipwreck

Three Chinese in yellow coats stood on dunes, waist-high
In the brittle grasses. They would be foreshortened
If anyone, some Margaret ghost, was looking inland
Where the snow
Was another catastrophe of quartz, a wanton sand,
Or so the oldest of them was thinking
While all three watched masts and sail,
Just sticks and a rag, being sucked into the Atlantic.

The bodies that washed up on shore were dressed
In nightshirts. They froze and the hair of the women
Snapped off at the scalp like glass.
The three Chinese had eaten opium:
The pellucid joints of the blue crabs
Were like the icy joints of the brittle grasses.

They watched it all, though it wasn't happening...

Their laundry and the Quail Island foundry
Vented together fire and steam. There were dragons
Dreaming everywhere. Irish from the furnaces
Came down the dunes
And rushed past the Chinese to the bodies on the beach.
The foreman stood in the water weeping.
His friends dragged him onto land,
And all seven walked toward the Chinamen
Who later, at dawn, were hanged with hotel sheets
Still warm from ironing.

So on her trip from Italy
Margaret Fuller and her child and husband were lost at sea.
Emerson sent Thoreau to comb the beach
For journals, clothing, or possibly

The rings. Emerson was patronizing
To her death. Hawthorne was vicious with care.
Henry James, the Master, said, "She was, at last,
Finally Italianized and shipwrecked." There were dragons
Feeding everywhere.

Safe Conduct

The snowplow was a rattling iron box
With a long chain sparking behind it.
The one curled blade raised to the air in Sanskrit.
The blue light on the floor of the cab
Was muted by a rag. The window, cracked
On my side, was sealed in the rose tint
Of a pinup from the garage.

The windshield wipers made time. The high beams
Failed in the night,
In the revealed light that is snow.
From the back of the truck Charlie Minor,
Who stood with a shovel in a mountain of rock salt,
Coughed and yowled. My grandfather shifted gears
And we began the descent to the country roads.

The blade dropped, the lip of a snarling dog.
Coming off the hill, going fifty,
We left the hard dirt that Parker plowed
And hit the drifting snow. Eight years old,
I reached into waxpaper
For chunks of ham, some cheese, and the red potatoes.
He laughed, a thermos of coffee in his hand;
Past midnight, he looked back
And I was asleep,
Propped up with a pillow of old surveyors' maps.
Charlie Minor drank from his pint of whiskey,
Yelling to my grandfather, "Sure is a bitch, Earl."
My grandfather adjusted his weight and put it to the floor.
The next morning his heart gave out.
In the barns we passed there were cows, each with a face
As distant as this world.

The Saints of Negativity

for Erma Pounds

It was the first snow in memory, and
A dark morning.
The cypress trees had fallen from the skies
Like long fan feathers of the white ibis.

The patron, Piero de' Medici,
Eating his orange,
Childishly summoned Michelangelo
Back to the villa
From the Infirmary of Santo Spirito
Where the sculptor
Had dissected a fresh body, his awful
Studies in anatomy.

A huge block of snow was shaded
With skins
And the young Michelangelo
Was to make a virgin and child.
Servants to Piero, as a joke,
Had spoiled the marble
With a trickle of ox blood. Then
They paved the uncarved block
With more snow and a glaze of water.

Under the afternoon sun
Michelangelo reached the courtyard
And the snowmen of Piero's bastard children
Had sagged into large pears
Which the hungry birds sat upon...

Piero de' Medici, disappointed with the sun,
Had gone to bed with his first cousin

Who as a girl
Had roasted and eaten her favorite falcon.

Still in his hospital apron
Michelangelo sat in the cart
With one hand on a muddy wheel
And stared into the white stubble
Of the distant field. All he could see

Was the bearded face of the old peasant
He had undone that same morning.
He took his wrap of knives
And approached the block of snow. He threw

Off the goatskins. He told Piero later
That a woman and child were buried in snow;
That he found them, but
In the sunlight they turned to water
And wine, possibly water and blood. He didn't
Know. Make no mistake, he said,
The earth like a crust of bread absorbed them.

The Desert Deportation of 1915

Our dead fathers came down to us in the river.
Thousands of fathers and grown brothers
Bobbing in the Euphrates...
The two generals rode their horses
Over the hill
Like happy widows on strong donkeys.

My mother loved men; I buried
Her in the river with them.
There was limitless mind in the open eyes
Of my dead mother.
I buried my little brother on the grass plain.
Dogs dug him up that night. At dawn
I buried him again—what
I could find of him—in excrement
Stolen from latrines.
The dogs would let him be. I stuck
Two dozen irises from the riverbank
In his grave, it all baked hard
In the sun that day.

One of the Turks, a cook,
Thought a little girl this smart
Should be saved.
I wish I could say they were
All cruel and disgusting.
But they gave me fruit and bread.
On the march down the valley
They left me with villagers
Who were of the Muslim faith. And
Though I was lazy, they raised me
From the dead.

Near the Bridge of Saint-Cloud

after Rousseau

A swollen infant under a tree, rose petals
Stuck to his cheeks, heavy plaster eyelids
Clucking like false teeth in disbelief...

He was abandoned here by his mother
Who is a student of the East.
At sunrise she thought the reflected
Arches of the bridge over the water
Were the brass-knuckles of the Turkish Police.

She knew the shaded riverbank was a street
For the serene bourgeoisie:
And the strolling painter
And the baby, who are
One and the same, openly
Look toward us
Rather than to each other,
Which would complete the painting.

The mother is now huddled in a yellow shack
In the middle of vineyards.
Her spoon in the candle flame blackens.
There's the last of the powder
On a square of paper
And a hose tourniquet the color of skin.
What she sees, unlikely muse

Inspiring mystery, is not the throne room
Of some sad Byzantine, but the metal
Bitch camel of King Artabanus:
The automaton would spit and kick, was musical
Beyond comprehension,

And its right-front hoof, studded with rubies,
Was used by the King to crush the skulls
Of family members who proved uninteresting.

Old Artabanus had a large ascending throne,
An elevator of gold flanked by palms.
It rose to a lapis dome
Which was eventually painted in the blood
Of another king's messenger-son
Who thought to promote a peace,
Equal to childhood, throughout the kingdoms of the East.

Amen

for Patrick & Robert

Someone calls *Duchess,* our fawn Great Dane, back
Across the dusty road: she's nearly to the lawn
When the Buick hits her, she rolls
And then gaining her legs
Runs into the field of goldenrod where my father
Finds her; when he presses
The large folded handkerchief against the wound, it vanishes
Along with his forearm. She was months dying.

One night returning from my aunt's house, we stopped
At a light and watched a procession of cars
Coming down out of the first snow, down
Out of the mountains, returning to Connecticut. Everywhere
Roped to the hoods and bumpers were dead deer.
The man behind us honked
His horn. My father waved him on. He hit
The horn again. My father got out and spoke
With him in a voice that was frightening
Even for a man with a horn. We left the door open
And the four of us sat there in the dome light
In silence. Wanting to be fair,
I thought of squatting cavemen, sparks flying
From flints into dry yellow lichen and white smoke
Rising from Ethel Rosenberg's hair.

Radio Sky

The blue house at Mills Cross
Where the night's last firefly
Strikes its light out in a burst pod.

Under the cool stairs
You raised the chrome visor
On my aunt's old G.E.:
A faint band, green numerals
And a backlighting of amber tubes —
Each is glass, prophylactic,
With cosmic noise straight from the Swan.

Your sister, Phyllis, had been unkind. It was hot.
Our towels floating in the tub upstairs,
We lit candles
And you poured the iced tea.

Later in bed you turned on the television
To where a station had signed off;
Making the adjustments in the contrast
We watched snow, what Phyllis said
Was literally the original light of Creation.
Genesis popping like corn in a black room. Still,
Something out of nothing. Knowing

We can't have children
You watched the flecked light
Like a rash on your stomach and breasts.
Phyllis

Is a bitch was my reply.
We made love, shared strings of rhubarb

Leached with cream. We slept
In the blue snow of the television
Drifting under the familiar worn sheet.

Coyote Creek

It was a small canyon, very small
With a low waterfall, saw-grass running
From the pool to the decaying ponderosa ridge.
The north wall, cut by water, was
Pure, almost tantric. The stream ran over a red floor.
The other wall had blue lichen on it.

A rope up in the juniper. Swallows nesting
In the north wall; they *were,* I thought,
The politics of the City of God. I told them
I wouldn't trouble their babies.
I said a prayer to this place
For a friend who had lost all hope.

I am not cautious. But when my daughter
Brought me a handful of chalcedony
I helped her return it to the mud pool
Below the juniper. I told her
It would have lost its colors in the air —
We are to disturb nothing here. *I have*

Said a prayer for John.
Just then a *scare-bird* with a white stripe
Across its wings and back,
Across the fan of its tail feathers, cried
Out from the barren ridge. It reminded me
Of a sack, black
With white bones painted on it
That belonged to my grandmother. What
Kept him on the ridge

Was a force of twelve swallows with young.
I walked up the sandy path

To where my daughter sat in the car.
She was angry. My wife comforted her. *We are*

To disturb nothing here. I had
Said a prayer to water and rock.
I had refused a gift from my daughter,
And watched
The *scare-bird* sing, shifting in the dead pines
While the sun sank all at once behind him.

Thomas Merton and the Winter Marsh

for Amiee

I went out of the house to smoke. A thousand
Buntings in the brown stalks, scolding
The sudden cold
That's come down from Canada
That rushes the clouds to illusion, an old moon
Behind them seems to plummet —

The fat yellow spider, out earlier with the thaw,
Lowers herself on silk that
Turns solid in the cold,
Surprising us both.
She tries to climb by eating the string of ice
But can't and waits —
I put my hand under her,
Scissors over rock, she drops
Into soft hands.

I bring her inside the house
And put her in the stone cupboard
That has no ceiling, that was
A chimney in another century. If

I am ever translated into sky
I will expect my spit to turn to ice
And I will eat it and rise, unlike

The yellow spider, like the brides
And mother of Christ.

Anagram Born of Madness at Czernowitz, 23 November 1920

There are still songs to sing
On the other side of mankind.

PAUL CELAN

They were the strong nudes of a forgotten
Desert outpost, crossing through snow
Through the steam of a hot springs
Where they bathed twice daily against delirium.

It was during the conflict between the Americans
And North Koreans. We realized
They would use atomic weapons.
Our eyes were alive and you could read them.

How out on the glaciers
Angels were burning the large brooms of sunflowers,
A backgrowth without smoke. Each flower's head,
An alchemist's sewer plate of gold.

They were coming down in winter
And whatever they were, Mr. Ancel's ghost
Would meet them,
Saying, "You may go this far and no farther."

Like fountains in winter the heart-jet
Is bundled in shocks of straw. Now, it's cold soldiers
In a swamp cooking a skull.
The harsh glazings in my room.

Grandmother ate a sandwich while dusting
A bone cudgel

In a beam of light
In the green cellar of the museum.

When the lard factory across the street
Began burning, soap tubs collapsing with the floor,
She said, quietly,
"There, see, we must have imagined the whole thing...

I don't hear the bells. Do you, children?
If there's an explosion, it will come as a wind
Peppered with things—
Hold on to me and we'll sing."

Tomb Pond

for Dave Smith

A farmer drags two lashed poles through a storm

While down the road in the snowy woods
Twelve mules are working on a tomb
For a drummer boy who was killed at Bull Run.
The farmer is wrestling two green poles.
He is building a scarecrow in the snow.
The drummer boy was his nephew. Later,

He will say that during that night
He suffered a slight stroke. It was
As if his left arm was slept upon, went numb,
And was strummed with a sensation
That did not include his thumb…

If there is a problem with the snow and the woods —
And, friend, there is —

Then, the destruction of an alphabet
Is the beginning of language.
It's as if some large stone
Is the cold horizon above the farmer
Erecting a scarecrow in a late-autumn storm.
The crows that watch him

Fear he has learned what they knew
All along, stealing his white corn. Alone
Too often in a room, we are open to reflection
As an old pond once built to solemnize a tomb.

A True Story of God

Henry Thoreau is lost in the Maine woods
At the center of the black pond
Standing in an Old Town canoe, his arms
Are raised welcoming a moose
Who is drunk with the methane
Of bottom grasses...

The moose was, in fact, already fatally shot
Through the nostril
By an Indian guide and companion
To the transcendentalist traveler
Now fainting back into his rented canoe
That is gliding toward the floundering moose—
The guide's knife

Has sliced off the upper lip of the creature
As a delicacy for his woman.
The long rubbery hairs of the lip
Will be burned away that night
At the large campfire
Where Thoreau is brooding, telling himself
That God is in nature and nature
Is in men; in that order, he thinks,
Lies the salvation of all animals
Who are placed closer to God than to humans.

Humans who, while knowing they possess a soul,
Become useless. Useless and cruel. Thoreau jumps,
The fat of the lip
Snapping from the flames like gunfire.

Revelation 20:11–15

for Tito

He was a farmboy who had drowned that Wednesday
While trying to swim two gray horses across the river.
We had met him once at the cemetery
Where our father was burying his aunt.
We had watched with him while two limousines, a pickup,
And a cab from Bath entered the gate. He looked
At the urn of African violets and then with his shoulder
Tipped it, riling some yellow slag-burning bees.
He laughed and ran past the trees toward the beach,
And the wildness of his arms and legs
Made me think he might be climbing a tall building.
But he was running away; slowing in the dunes,
He was still in sight even as we were dragged
To our mother by the enraged deacon Blaisdale.
He said we were common vandals.
You were silent. I said
That little shit Smithy had done it.
We began crying. Miss Rose, who had witnessed everything,
Crossed the lawn to save us from judgment.
Deacon Blaisdale began apologizing, our mother
Interrupted him with what would happen
If ever again he laid hands on either of us—
By now the Smith boy jumping into the Atlantic—
In my heart I thanked him for bringing
Down the righteous six-foot deacon
Who was going very red in the face as our own mother
Slapped me for calling the dead boy a name.
Well, he wasn't dead yet, but when he was
We were amazed.

A Depth of Field

for David St. John

The trailer, a bubble of aluminum and glass,
One hundred of them in a field
Beside the poplars and the frozen lake—
Everywhere else tennis courts, some
With the nets still there, the posted
Snow fences of another place, wind and heavy ice
In general for miles...

It's there, in the weather, my father chews his cigar
At the old scrivener's bench,
A first-year medical student in my mother's apron
Dissecting a black cat, daubing
At the wide trench.

I look down through the curb of the skylight
And see it all, the whole sum
Of a winter landscape sucked into the open cat
Like a red sock into the vacuum.

When you faint there *is* a sudden tunneling.
There is also the smell
Of smoke and formaldehyde on your father's shirt.
And while you wake, for that instant,
There are white monkeys at all the gates.

Looking up from Two Renaissance Paintings to the Massacre at Tiananmen Square

Fruit flies lift off the bowl of brown pears.
The volume of the television is turned down.

If you watch Christ raise Lazarus from the dead
You will observe that he is always
Upwind of him. The unfortunate
Sisters are downwind
With bags of cloves pushed to their faces.
Olive trees, on the dry hillside, lean
In these famous paintings, leaving the direction
Of the wind not in question.
Christ, if you believe the Italians,
Was like most white magicians —

Clean and well positioned.
It's summer, supper is finished
Except for its odors. Before dusk begins
There's an hour of strong light
Which would never offend the religious.
It's in this light
That I look up at the bleached screen.
There, in the silence, students fall before machines.
It's as if they are the faint
Of a mass healing. In a suburb of the city
There is a mound of bodies which will be burned.

But death is a bearded man spilling
From a coffin, dressed in a black gown;
In Tehran, if death is a woman, then her hem
Will drag over the ground.

Confession

for Hank

The General's men sit at the door. Her eyes
Are fat with belladonna. She's naked
Except for the small painted turtles
That are drinking a flammable cloud
Of rum and milk from her navel.

The ships out in the harbor
Are loosely allied
Like casks floating in bilge.
The occasional light on a ship
Winks. In the empty room of the manuscript
Someone is grooming you
For the long entrance into the dark city.

They'll hang the General.
Then with torches they'll search for his children.
Men and women
Are seen jumping from the burning hotel.
Journalists, in no hurry,
Elect to take the elevator. They walk
Out of the building, stepping over corpses...
You are listening to loud bells.

The corpses get up and follow the journalists.
It's unfair that while rehearsing
For death they actually succumbed to it.
But no one sobs.
Shirts and dresses billowing as they fall.
Something inhuman in you watched it all.
And whatever it is that watches,
It has kept you from loneliness like a mob.

The Diatribe of the Kite

for Khenpo Karthar Rinpoche

They come from the white barrier of noon
Where two forces of magnetism, one weak
And one strong, combine
To create a cruel sea of iron filings
Over which, as unlikely pilgrims, they journey.

As our sun rises, and they sleep,
Only then do they become
The ancestors of whom we are ashamed.

These two behemoths, one red and one green,
Sulk over willow sticks, rice paper,
And a wooden pot of glue. There is gold leaf
Like raked fire between them.

They swallow blood with milk. They feast
On the roasted tongue of prisoner angels.

When they nap, in the late afternoon,
The earth moves... They wake
Like simple accordions. And they are doomed.
Much of what they know, they learned
While grazing in the field with animals.

Their kite will be flown in a storm. It is
The crossed sticks of punishment
Above the city
Of their making. In time, they have taken

Two names: *Yang Baibing, Deng Xiaoping.*
In rhyme, they are joyously insane.

They are the immortality of the nursery
Where they reign —
Those ancestors for whom we are ashamed.

The Evening of the Pyramids

for Kim

A summer night in the desert is as welcome
As the savant in robes
Who's come to build an aqueduct of stone.
Here, the night will not support ghosts.
They visit at noon
And at the poles of twilight.
The red caftans of the angry horsemen
Float on the distant skyline

Where date palms are blistered gold. The birds
Who eat from these trees
Mistake the air for alcohol. In a hot wind
The dusty postal road is lined with palms,
Their dried fruit a storm of castanets.
And then suddenly there's silence…

The Sphinx was to the backs of the Frenchmen
Deployed in squares: at the centers
Napoléon placed large cannon, donkeys
Loaded with provisions,
And two hundred scholars he found
In a heavy winter conscription.
A single lengthening report of rifle fire
Left six thousand Mameluke horses
Dying on their sides like fish.
The Mameluke men were stripped, emptied into the Nile.
The smell of gunpowder
Wafted into the slums of Cairo.

The next evening, Bonaparte
In the Pyramid of Cheops asked to be left
In the King's Chamber, empty

But for the sarcophagus of granite
Cut at the original site of Atlantis.

When Napoléon left the tomb
For daylight, he was visibly changed
But would say nothing of what he'd seen.
The very same room had shaken
Both Alexander and Caesar.
Even when dying, at Elba, he persisted
In repeating, "You would not have believed it.
Is it evening?"

The Emperor said nothing.
What he saw can be reported faithfully,
And its significance is plain —
There was a dark room and an empty coffer for a king.

A Dream of Three Sisters

From night rocks, above an ocean alive with yellow kelp,
The ghost of Samuel Taylor Coleridge tossed
Raw chunks of a disquieting muse
To three ragged mermaids... each
Had a long tooth the white of gruel.
Coleridge knelt in his velvet coat
With a prune-dark dog
Who barked at the sagging breasts of the women.
When the sisters stopped tearing at their meat
To scowl back at the benefactor, the dog
Would whimper under the silks of a tent
In which he and Coleridge slept
Like evangelists of a new forbearance.
Two old philosophers not troubled by death
Like the moon Phobos, which rises and sets
Twice each day above this martian landscape.
Here, the ghost of Coleridge sat, fully disconsolate,
With little more than thought for the fatal opiate...
But how, you must ask, exactly did that dog
Become spirit? It was a winter day
On a small farm in Massachusetts.
White-winged horses were feeding like geese
From the very bottom of a pond placed among trees.
The dog was to be shot that morning by the farmer Smith
Who shot himself instead. His wife
Drowned the mongrel the next day
In a sack filled with nails for weight.
The dog was not sick. It was rumored
He had killed her cat. It was in this manner
That a mongrel entered the esteemed company
Of the addict Coleridge.
The afterlives of the gentle farmer and cat
Are an open subject. Perhaps

They live on the happy side of the same ocean
That is a torment to the dog and poet.
They were the first to burst upon this lonely sea.
They often wonder what it must be like
Being wholly ordinary.

Homage to Philip K. Dick

for Paul Cook

The illegal ditch riders of the previous night
Will deliver ice today.
The barbers up in the trees are Chinese.
They climb with bright cleats, bearing machetes—
It's a season
Of low self-esteem for date palms on the street.

My visitor was at the door yesterday.
In a blue sere of a sucker suit.
An *I Like Ike* button
On the lapel. Holding a cup of sawdust.
He breathed through his eyes, crusted
With pollen.

I was not confused. It was God
Come to straighten my thoughts.
Whole celestial vacuums
In the trunk of his pink Studebaker.
He would smoke and cough.
I sat very still, almost at peace with myself.

He had shot a deer in the mountains. He thought
Last year's winterkill was worse than usual.
I told him I didn't know about guns.
Something forming on his forehead—a gloriole
Of splattered sun over snow.
We drank our lemonade in silence.

He asked if he could go. He joked
About his wife's tuna casserole. As a gift
I signed for him my last paperback.
He left the book of matches. I'll not enroll

In the correspondence course it offers
For commercial artists. What a relief

That the barbers in the trees are Chinese.
Green fronds are dropping in twos and threes
Around the bungalow, lessons
In the etiquette of diseased parrots. Bill Cody
Said it first, "If there is no God, then I am
His prophet." Stop it. Please stop it.

Inside the City Walls

A small boy in shock with a blue Popsicle
In the dark hallway of a Montreal hospital—
His mother floats past me
Away from the nurses' station,
Her dead husband's silver glasses in her hand
Exactly as I had learned to hold the javelin:
The first position,
Arm trailing while the wrist turns,
Thumb in rebellion, the whole body
Mindless of its gathering speed, head lolling
Impossibly, the spear
Is pulled from the chest
Where the foot is first firmly planted...

The Bus Stopped in Fields of Misdemeanor

for Brittony

I don't know why they turn the irrigation
On the oranges before they are frozen.
And you are not my daughter, but my daughter's friend.
Your mother is dead in Los Angeles.
Charles Dickens, dying,
Dreamt of large workhorses
With flaring tinctured gums
Charging down a mountain of fine white powders...
It meant nothing to him. It was a blessing.

Forgive me, in the middle of all this,
If I ask your pardon. The newspapers
Report an icy canker in the orchards.
The growers are alarmed but optimistic.

It is a winter morning in the desert. I woke
To one of those heavy trains of language:
It's Hannah's friend, Brittony, her mother's dead
From an overdose of heroin.
I honestly don't know why
It bothered me so much, it's almost out of season
And I am of the enemy. And we are legion.

Two Women on the Potomac Parkway

On Tuesday's bus I heard the man from State
Describe for his mistress
How soldiers in Ethiopia
Raped an eleven-year-old shepherdess...
Muriel, I swear he thought
It would turn her on. I told Sam
She probably *did* shred paper with the best of them.

We saw that photograph on television.
It looked like Reptile Man
Dressed in enema bags. You know
The other one with two men in leather jackets —
It reminded Sam of the boy in Maine
Who rode his motorcycle along our pines
And into a black half-acre hatch of mayflies.
The bike dragged him down the mountain highway,
A thousand bugs
Like live soot in his mouth and nostrils.
It made Sam sad. He thought Mapplethorpe
Was gifted. Two of our children
Dead in as many years.

Look how the snow has drifted
Up to the slats on that fence. It's like the dirty
French postcards you buy in museums now.
The snow is brazen.
Mr. Lincoln sitting there above it all.
Mr. Lincoln's Tad, who suffered a cleft palate,
Died not long after his father was martyred.

From Tuesday's bus I saw three congressmen
In fur coats. They were waiting for the light to change.
The fat one's hat blew off,

His cronies laughing at him. Doubled over
He began to wade across the lawns; finally
Up to his waist in drifts, just half a man
Dressed in animal skins, he reached
Into that vast pornography of snow
And rescued his hat and honor. It wasn't funny, Muriel.
It made me sick, if you must know.

Psalm XXIII

It was the first Wednesday of a scarcity of candles.
The planes, of course, came in waves. They came
With the dinner bell. Only Eric
Remained upstairs. Inside the orange room
Plaster settled on everyone and in the soup.
Outside snow fell
Heavily around our houses. In the garden
The broken water pipes gushed and froze
Over a horse whose backside was crushed by fallen bricks;
The heated water hissed and as the horse
Took on ice, still propped up with its forelegs,
It stood like a feeding mantis, the awful mouth
Open around its swollen tongue.
We dipped our napkins in the thin soup
And, draping them over our faces, walked
Out into the smoke. The munitions factory
On the hillside blossomed and burned. It was earsplitting,
And sudden. I got sick.
In shame, I went back inside, changing into Father's pajamas.
Uncle shot the horse; it shattered,
A fallen chandelier with all its candles white,
Save one red tier.
Eric remained upstairs, more out of disgust
Than fear.
We had a car, and had hoarded petrol.
In the morning
We would drive to the Swedish Legation.
Mother said that on a burnt-out building,
With chalk, someone wrote: *Lily, the Aunt was killed.*
I have room now I think
For both you and the children. Where are you?
When there's snow on the ground
The automobiles, lorries, and trains are very plain to see

And the bombers have a field day.
Men pass mornings scattering ashes
Around the factories and in Soldiers' Cemetery
Where the Americans bomb mercilessly. Out in the garden
The homeless cut great steaks from the sides
Of Uncle's dead horse.
Uncle thought this both practical and wholesome.
But when they dragged out its intestines
He shot above their heads and cursed them.
They ran in the direction of the park.
Father wanted to know if there was anything
Eric wanted. He said that to start with
He'd drop a bomb on that horse's carcass
And have it done with…
Father said everyone was nervous
And Eric could go to his room until breakfast.
I saw him once again
That evening in a coffin.

A Renunciation of the Desert Primrose

for J. Robert Oppenheimer

I am tired of the black-and-white photograph
Of a government bunkhouse, tin and pine,
And the orchids in the catalpa trees
Shriveled to twine. A white birdcage
Hangs from a rafter.
This was the sleep of mathematics, the poor facts
Of primrose. An MP struts
With a large sack filled with rattlesnakes.
The tar-paper windmill kneels out in the dunes,
Battered hat of the Pilgrims.
Beside the bunkhouse,
A tower and checkpoint. Again, a large sack
Slack with mind. The head of the Medusa inside.
Across the dunes
Dead flowers scatter like X rays of the thorax.
I have fallen behind...

A Blue Hog

I didn't have to buy the acid.
I found it in an old battery in the barn
Where the cows make sea noises
And the cobwebs are plated gold.
There were packets of birdseed, white floats
Of cork, turpentine, and an old black fishline
Which shouldn't have worked but did.
All of it a sin for the taking—
I chose the acid for its smoke
And the fishline to tie around my toe
To remind me of the smoke.
I threw the rotten apples into the yard
And the blue hog charged.
He was unpardonable, having
Killed my sister's child. John couldn't
Butcher him — *to eat that hog*
Would be to eat the child.
I poured the acid into pink Christmas bulbs
And sewed them into the hollowed apples.
I put them out into the sun to soften.
The hog swallowed them whole like smoke.
By the time he looked under himself
He was already broke. My long dress shook.
He stopped to give me a look,
And then ran straight at the barn.
His head and shoulders passed through the boards.
The horse inside
Had a hissing fit over him. Nobody
Has ridden that horse since
Except for the devil
Who's said to still be in the district.

Margaret's Speech

I'm a frogman. Naked by the water
Under a lean of canvas she'd sewn
With a thick paraffin thread,
She gestured. *When we pulled him*
From the river
His left leg was meal. Crayfish in the hair.
The river bottom left his shoulder
Layered and crocheted—
My sister's pearl knitting needles
Clicking in my head. I told
The sheriff I wouldn't do it again.

I knew him once. His Chevy threw a rod.
I made it with him
On the hood of the old truck.
It was out at the dump beyond Yuma.
It felt like I had bread crumbs
All over my mouth. Wacky with the sun,
I sure did it with him enough
That afternoon. I didn't

Know it was him who'd drowned.
They said it was his cousin.
He had a three-cornered scar
At the small of his back. And a deposit
Of calcium on the tailbone.
We're not much, you know?

He was tangled in yellow tree roots,
He spun in the currents,
A fishhook and line running
From his thumb.
A whole new ball of wax, I thought.

I wanted to be an astronaut.
But failed the mathematics
Twice in one summer.
So I raise Nubian goats.
My favorite has a purple manure
That comes out like steaming packets
Of tobacco mulch. He sprays
The shack with his seed—
It hasn't needed paint in three years.

I just took my shorts off
When you two came down the hill.
It's that rubber suit I wear
When I dive into the chute and cave.
Sometimes I just feel
Like old air in a patched tire. Then,
I get my Seagram's and come out here.
You two look married. Not that I care.
You wouldn't believe what I was just thinking—
Your husband's the only living man
Left in this county
Who knows that I bleach my hair.

Bellevue Exchange

The ground on which the ball bounces
Is another bouncing ball.

DELMORE SCHWARTZ

A large man rowing in a white tub
While the fog sweeps over him
And the orange pines of the island
Reflect everywhere in the brightly tiled room.
The red shell of the razor clam
And a cup of soap rest on a fresh towel.

He lowers his head, moose moving like his genitals
Through the room, he steps out onto the water—
He hears the telegraph of glass beads, the decades
Of drowned nuns traveling to Quebec. Now
A yellow rain like straw piercing the lake.
A long narrow waist in conflict

With large breasts and hips, she crosses
The room with both hands on the full glass
Of bourbon. He reaches through the fog for it,
And a bell from land
Cancels everything. Towels tossed
To the floor. The water climbing for him.

Simple Philo of Alexandria

You will see what is behind me
But my face will not be seen by you.

EXODUS 33:23

For what are we to think? But that Philo
Goaded his rich merchant brother Lysimachus
Into selling winecasks, jewels,
And all his servants
To finance a projectile to the moon.

Philo's friends, brothers in the dark prospect,
Gathered with the Emperor's mistresses
Just below Nero's courtyard
Where the red rocket wrapped in straw
Sat in its brass caution of gunpowder.

With burning cane Philo ignites
The fuse, which is a braid of human hair.
The rocket climbs like a goose
Breaking out of the water, flying
Through the fire of outbank ether.

It veers into the carts of Charlemagne
And having lost its course, passes our moon —
A seer of Nero's watches the projectile
Cross the orbits of planets,
Through a storm of chalk and bones,
Passing out of the Cosmos…

Now eternal in its voyage,
It blazes away from the venue of the seer,
Which was thought to be nearly absolute.
It does not return to its Emperor, burning

Most of Rome.
It keeps on going—insubstantial, a spirit vehicle,

It begins to compose itself,
For the very first time, inside the mind of Philo
Who is one soul
Among the incalculable number of souls,
All as inseparable
From simple Philo as from the whole.

November 23, 1989

after Blake

Two rising flukes of green water
Joined and fell like marble
On the black ships which tipped
And sunk. A gull was thrown against the sky.
The cloaked men and women on the cliff
Watched the clouds in darker battery
Move against the very ground of sea.
The water is a turning page of scripture
Pleased with the impossible needs
Of pilgrims who stood arranged in disbelief.

It is the Thursday of a certain need
That must yet become more desperate
If wilderness is to be raised above itself
Like fire in the airshafts of a skyscraper.

What if in some long thanksgiving
They refused as friends to be ordinary company
And instead thought of themselves
As the eventual dead.
Then, the wattle fence made to limit geese
Would collapse and become the skids of memory
Gone beyond Babylon
Into crowded streets where hooves
Of horses sparked with simple symmetry
Like those biggest bones that by necessity
Must bear away the most meat.

In the Time of False Messiahs

circa 1648

He sat in the shade of trees at moonrise
Following with his eyes the tracks of fleas
Who were hunting wolves. A poor rabbi
Dressed in a paper gown, he ate a black potato.
Women danced behind him like the snow.
There were boats in the sky above him
And they were lowering ropes.
There was famine everywhere in Poland.

The fires of the city made him cold
So he walked into the forest.
He walked along a brook into the hills.
He praised the white trees
And the owls that nested in them:
Their simple fires of digestion, the bones
Of mice igniting in their bowels.
He reached up and grasped a rope.
He climbed into the boat.
There was famine everywhere in Poland.

Everywhere below him there was hope.

A Physical Moon Beyond Paterson

for Brian

William Carlos Williams had finished
His mid-December rounds
In an old hospital made of fieldstones.
He walked out into the late-afternoon sun
And sat in his car, an emerald Hudson.
He said *no* twice and straightened,
The car slowly going down the rural hill.
He saw a row of technicians dressed in lead coats
And yesterday's baby with a bowel obstruction.
All of the previous night
This road was plowed. The snow
Climbing six feet now on either side.
With little warning a hot spike
Had entered his elbow. He had suffered a stroke.
Maybe he was lost for oxygen: some odd gaiety
Overwhelmed him while descending a winter hill.
He began to play the green Hudson
Violently against the two walls of snow,
Leaving the seasonal paint of the car
On a quarter mile of water turned crystal.
Accelerating, he shot across the state highway
Coming to rest in a marsh with a deep brook.
He was crying and singing, awake
With the spongy earth below him.
He was not the Polish woman of his night-calls:
She endured two hours of labor
Scouring her kitchen floor. She curtsied
And froze, delivering in that position
A seven-pound girl.
And that's the glory. For a moment
This old man was a rough sluice of toboggan
Gone tobogganing.

And then he just walked out across
The colossal toxic wilderness of New Jersey,
The holiest dish to whiteness passing over...

PART TWO
Poems 1991 – 2001

I saw blood on the horn of the moon.

PADMASAMBHAVA

The Urgrund does not advertise
to the artifact that is here.

PHILIP K. DICK

The Mercy Seat

He sat in an enamel tub with a black
Palm tree beyond the window. While he was dying
There in the cold bath
Flaming arms closed down around him,
The weighted wings of seraphim
Were milling the heart out of the long arc
Of covenants. It is what saves him.

In great wind and rain he once watched
Thousands of white snails
Fall from high fronds across the boulevard.
The Mercedes left the road
And struck a goat, its blood
Ran to the sick marsh
Like a line of pink gasoline that's burning.

There's a black-and-white Polaroid
Of his mother
Where the continuous elastic of her undergarment
Leaves a colorless band
That wraps around her lower ribcage
Descending to the abdomen. We will need

Now to discuss flowers.

The postman tells him more bundled children
In Croatia have seen the Virgin Mary.
In mirrors mostly, but one girl
Dressed in a red wig, who has suffered
Radium therapy for weeks, saw
The Blessed Mother's dress
Substitute itself for a green transformer
High on a telephone pole
That was humming out across the evening snowstorm. And

That's all the good news there was,
Except for today he climbed the grassy knoll
To stand silently with three men in hats —
They were surveying the ocean for boats
While he was content to settle on the facts...

Elegy for My Brother

I'll walk awhile, maybe as high as the tree line—
The tick-infested heads of those deer, their silhouettes
Over the field, gave me courage somehow
To speak with you. I awoke, did
You know, just as you died. Later I was told
That it rained quietly all over Manhattan.
Neon, even in rain, is a crippled light.
I awoke from a dream of irregular snowfields
Where all the white lampshades
Were taken away; regained as blood-soaked orchids—
April's lady's slipper: labial, alien—these supernumerary
Flowers were being eaten by mule deer. Mozart's
Requiem K. 626 turning to snow
While being broadcast weakly from deep inside Canada...

The cold river has a lashing movement like cilia
And we can see our breath in the air. The lit rooms.
Robert, where are your shoes?
What was it that haunted Pierce House? All the way
Down that oak hall to an unheated bathroom
Which we were asked to share
With four other families of poor divinity students.
Who was it, me or you, who first realized
We could reach the kitchen sink and pee into it?
I have a memory where I am watching wind
Fall deliberately, at night, over the red carriage barn.
There is lightning sickness in the trees. Everything's thawing.
You're there, at the windowsill, with me. The storm windows
Begin rattling, great sheets of ice
Fall from the slate roof like blades.
We pretend the house is a guillotine.
You say we must save the life of an aristocrat's maid. You say,
Giggling, that she is knock-kneed.

Once we waited outside on the porch
Knowing our ears were badly frostbitten. Mother had
Warned us of how it would hurt
When eventually we returned to a warm place. You rubbed
Snow on both our ears and we just stared at the colored shocks
Of Indian corn our father had nailed to the door.
You begged me to stay out longer.
I would have actually left you there...
                                        but now
I am still preparing to leave, to return
To a heated kitchen where dried marigolds stab the ceiling.

We were just two boys contemplating a wooden door.
It's getting colder. Mozart's heavy Sanctus turning to snow.
Then you smile at your feet, laugh,
Run up into the orange light that spills
From the opening door. The requiems are melting back into music.
I stand in snow
And watch the door now being closed behind you...

At the Death of a Mongolian Peasant

for L.J.

The trees turned around as if to quarrel with him.
To stay warm
The old man had raked the hen yard,
There was some rote of ferociousness
In the wind entering the marsh grasses.
Grasses dryly caked with clay,
Making an immense broken plane of pipes and rattles.

Wild geese flew over the yellow cottage
In twos and threes. They screamed
To the old man in simple allegiance to need.

The radio crackles away on the white cupboard—
The last voice of the Supreme Soviet
Joins the thrashing grasses that surround the cottage.
I laugh. This wet night is a fifties bassinet...

Brightly colored decals of fat rattlesnakes
Plastered all over it...
                           it is a hot,
Almost incandescent, trailer park in Mesa, Arizona.
So the old peasant snores

Beyond even the fear of *that* new morning.

Has he endeared himself to the dark?

It is the wind's ventriloquism
That talks down a long straw to him; he listens
Floating, at cyc-level, out over the wild rice,

Now colored iodine by a late moon. What he lisped
Was the frantic accusation of leaves. What he gets,
    from a worldly perspective,

Is a cold rain that begets still more rain,
And some simple wretchedness unto bliss.

A Skeleton for Mr. Paul in Paradise

after Allan Guisinger

In the fine cataracts of falling mountain water,
A large assembly of yellow bones,
A moose with tattered black armbands
Hanging from the darker branches of its rack...

Your neighbor's heart has a winter's hole in it.

He sits straddling
A beast of calcium with velvet slough —
Posit here the museum's tin of lacquer,
Paste, and wire, or the red wiggling
Of an india ink. This dream, though,

Is the public viewing —

The way the neighbor becomes proud, rising slightly
Off the lumens of the creature, an air
Exemplary to any desperate cavalry of bones.

He peers down over the waterfall. There
In the settled water of fallen things
Is the brighter composition:
                                    his dead sisters,
And a mother who waits, knowing
It is not a cleared cadaver of the forest
That is his white mount, but rather
A weighted nostalgia for robes and boats. Or

Just the dead neighbor, still living, peering in at your window
While you wake, saying:

Can I have some of your meal and leaves
For my worms; after dark, I'm going out to the lake—
There are eels spawning
Where the shoals meet the snowmelt and yesterday's rain.

And you wake again,

Then he screams meaninglessly,
Wearing the mask of a child who drowned
While dressed in ice skates and the long green gown.

A Fifteenth-Century Zen Master

for Stephen

A blind girl steps over the red staves
Of a tub. Steam rising from her shoulders and hair,
She walks across a dirt floor to you.
I think you are not her grandfather.
You watch with her a pink man
Who has avoided taxes for two winters —
He is being judged by roosters
And has been chased this far into the countryside. Above him

Burning sacks of bat dung are arranged
In the purple branches of the thistle trees.
The river is indifferent to him.
And so are we.
You tell your mistress the burning bags of shit
Are like inert buddhas
Dissolving in a field of merit.

She giggles. A front tooth is loose.
With the river bottom clear as the night air,
The bargeman sings through the hungry vapors
Rising *now* like white snakes behind him.
You told his wife that Lord Buddha made wasps
From yellow stalks of tobacco with a dark spit.

Down in the cold bamboo a starving woman
Has opened a small pig —
The old moons climb from its blue glistening stomach,
Or is it light
From the infinitely receding sacks of shit?

Master, where is the difference?

The Caste Wife Speaks to the Enigmatic Parabolas

The two stonebreakers in loincloths
Have put aside the pickax and iron broom,
Are rolling an oildrum weighted with cement
Over the immaculate orbits
Of a white feldspar accident, stonefields
Flung from the throat of Cygnus: a fire of hydrogen
Like ghosts of perfectly circumspect suns
Collapsing into oblivion. Holding

My husband's seed in my mouth, I walk
Out to his mother's pond and sink to the bottom—
Seed rises slowly from between my teeth:
Cap of salted milk, dead lily
Above me, or the dried birth caul of skin
That a pilgrim carries with him
To fend off ghouls, influenza, and the many
Sundry deaths by drowning.

Settled, my breasts lift with the green waters,
I am some rounded syllable lodged
In the brain of the contented sleeping child,
A trail of mother's milk drying on its shoulder
Leads to the fully opened cloak of a cobra
Motionless in shade
Whom the now awakened child pokes at with a stick,
Laughing and dancing in her place…

My husband's prick is an instrument of inscription
That has brought us to this banyan shade

Where the child on her side breathes, flutters
Imperceptibly: dropped cipher of a race

Of lightly colored men whom I now exchange
Gladly like blood for wine, like water
For the rising cream that forms a golden brick of butter.

Ghosts on the Northern Land of Ur

circa 2100 C.E.

With bits of pale colored chalk
My wife has made a pious study of this fire of rhododendron:
A very few branches, hunk of yak fat,
And a whole brick of dung. She points
To the red coral lake deep in the wasteland
Surrounded by orange fields of borax,
And the rusted machines are
Littering the sad alkali shades… more snow
In the box-trees; then, the wall of canvas
Set against the west winds: she hated
This lurid passage through time
And told us
We should dress for the glaciers
Where once she'd sold her body with rime.

Madame 'Xiang began to cry.

The tea is gone. There are herbs
For her mother's neck. A poultice of goose skin,
Some flour and cold mustards.
She was blind, I think, before joining the Lhasa expedition.

Above, the standard mandala of airships and the taxis; dirigibles
Like blue farts on the horizon. The clanking
Of the diesel airships has frightened the children
Though the fever dulls our hearing; one
Voice whispers to my wife about our dying in the night
And that seems right, my vision
Of a procession away from the hospital tents:
The convulsing legs
Of several hundred teams of starving oxen
Plowing through snow to make

A way for the bearers, their green poles
Splintering in the cold wind. She sings
While applying tree gum to the hem of her apron.

The loudest of the airships drops gliders from the belly
Like happy trout and then the venting of hot diesel
Scalds a dozen oxen: here
Begins a stampeding to the yellowing cliff
Where, by teams, they are falling
While a quarter of a mile below
The water is freezing to the blue heel of an escarpment.
The west wind carries the cries of these poor beasts
Who are still falling now, far below to the work camps
And first glaciers.

We thought we would go to the South, there is
Rioting in the coastal cities —
But with the deaths of half the oxen
The litters are put down by ranks in snow,
I heard them coughing for hours
Before they had all froze. It snowed some more

And that was their burial. I recognized
It was a dream when lame 'Xiang at first light
Went out with the Red Cross.

Their dirigibles were freshly stocked before the rains.
She found the wretched pile of broken oxen
Had softened with the balance of the storm, snow
Leaving the astonishing figure of Chenrezi:
Bodhisattva of their children's intrigues, bodhisattva
Of compassion, with a thousand arms

And a modest gold bodice like the orange brick
Chimney of some isolated Mongolian monastery.

In the crosswinds an Arab's parachute opens and descends,
The Gurkhas from their firing-nest open — the fogbank is
Marbled first with long threads of his stomach blood
And then a whole flood of it over the mind, its plateau
And glaciers...

I hallucinated — what, —
A supper bell and two dogs barking in the cold. The Panchen Lama

Is dead.
In 'Xiang's fever she prayed to the master of ceremonies
In a neon-bright holographic cabaret
For simple soup and rice.
And ice to the back of the leg.
All of which she got on the next watch
When Crow Woman, the "spring nurse," arranged

Our needs out of my wife's ravings. The witch
Had black mantras and a silver bell on her heavy keys
Which kept hungry ghosts out of the peach orchards. And
Her brother, she insisted, could squirt blood from his eyes
Like lizards.

In the old shrine room the silk brocade
Climbed thirty feet in wide banners
Above a blue topknot.
The souring butter lamps
Nourished thousands of active mice
Which gave the brocades a silver muscle of life —

Now the *nagas* move in the stream outside.

The smoke from the flesh-colored incense closes my eyes
While I chant like Grandfather taught me
On account of my wife's illness having become blood. My mind
Turns down in spiraling rows

Of even whiter blossoms
While over the hills I hear the small pig

That is still being slaughtered in our childhood...

After Sky X

Sky Z, in disbelief, agrees that this alphabet
Of mysteries was, one day, to reach him.

He was said, in a foolish legend of weather, to be
A husband of language
Like sudden lightning
Revealing the bare branches of a tree.

A complacency of owls in that same tree
Climbs to a night sky

Which is Z.

The revolving eyes of these owls
Like the changing aureoles of a woman's breasts
Guttering now into eternity.

Z establishes a rainbow of needs
Which is the only breach in eternity. He is
Searching for Sky A, who, in a discretion
Of letters substituting for lovers, forgets
The origin of rain and alphabets. Forgets

That Z is soon to forsake her—not
For the braille points of rising skin
Encircling the dark nipples of her breasts,

But, in the language of the deaf, for a signing
Of hands, which begs
That none of this be said.

The Photographer's Annual

1.

We are returning to New England for two weeks! My sister
Is having her wedding. She has asked for saguaro seeds.
The ironwood trees in the desert outside my window
Are silver, and from a distance are like the winter trees
Around my father's parsonage in New Hampshire.

His black garden has a palisade of dead sunflower stalks.
A little sister, among all the sisters,
Seems nearer to life, but lost. She eats a lettuce leaf
While gazing at a picture of school children boarding
A steamer in Odessa, circa 1933. She asks, "What happened
In this country? Can you guess the rest of their lives?"
And, not answering, I say with a smile, *"Mrs. Willow,
Where are your children? It's midnight! Ta-ta! Mrs. Willow?"*
(I tell her it's bedtime.) A kiss,
And then she climbs the stairs singing. I'm left

Looking sideways at the faces of Jewish children
Who are walking up a plank for a steamer-excursion
Out along the brink. A bright summer day!
Their almond eyes and all their white hands waving good-bye:
They are like spotted bean seeds, or a mass of frogs' eggs
Wiggling out in the pond under the blue sky.

We fear for children. Having been afraid all our lives.
I've sold two nudes. There's money now for wedding gifts.
For baked trout in that village diner.
There's the birch forest I want to photograph.

I have taken a Matisse, *La Blouse Romaine,* a poster
Reproduction, and cut out the face, skirt, and blouse.

My wife wore it with a breast showing through and
What a mask and costume it is; these photographs are the best
This month. It's not a parody. It's the truth! The more
We romanticize, the more removed we are from ourselves
And just that much closer to destruction.
The common peasant blouse is all the guilt there is in my
Subject — and then the breast pops out like
In a Frederick's garment
And what you hear is a little laughter between Lexi and myself

In our otherwise quiet house. It is a parody of thought, not
Of a peasant blouse, but of a life that's a wooden spoon and pot.
So my sister will marry a farmer. I am jealous.
And I continue: daydreams, the pictures, poems. My diary

Opens. The last day in New England I'll visit the pond
Inside the birch wood. Below the silver trees,
In the water, the frogs' eggs will glimmer and respond.

I'll imagine that they have no problems,
Not like the hounds in the distance
Calling after a rabid fox;

The fox who dipped his red chest
Into the pond. Who drank

The clear water. And who ate the green frog.

    II.

The black lustrous glyphs at the portals to a Mayan well
In the desert: below the ciphers there's a handsome goatherd
With a stiff green penis — a self-portrait —
Not very large except for a moment each year as the sun falls
In along the arroyo and shadow increases it!

To some degree, for centuries, this man in a scene with
Two goats becomes larger than himself. Is great art like this?

I'll admit that this portrait is a figure for longing.
But the theme here is not the loneliness of sex.

You want to know a secret?

The Mayan society had a few select nomadic members: women
With sheep and men with goats, and they wandered with never more
Than a day's travel separating them. (But they were also
Forbidden to meet.) Well, this goatherd's drawing
Was seen first, by design, in the late evening: the shepherdess
Fetching well water. There's a lamb bouncing at her feet.
The goatherd's erection directed her
Like a finger pointing out into the desert: South-southeast.
And when the other girls were asleep she went
South by southeast
Until she smelled equally—goats and sheep. She stopped
And right before her, proud and naked, stood
Her goatherd boy!

She smiles. A lizard stumbled over a dove's nest.
It must have been fun—*an arrangement*, all of the natural things,
And the sun for an accomplice.
I think all great art is erotic, secretive like maps,

And asks for the sun's forgiveness,
Asks for the sun as some confederate who will understand,
And, at the appointed moment, thoughtfully turn his back.

III. MY GRANDFATHER WHO LOVED PAINTINGS

I remember the children leaping inside the circle!

There were the wildflowers in clay: my head
Like them is opened and red.

My grandfather, a quarryman, raises me up off
The hard court and then we begin to climb
The iron stairs up the sheer tenement wall.
He was crying. And as if
This were a magical story: there's a veil
Of blood from the cut in my hair dripping
To the ground; no matter how fast he climbed
The veil played out more of itself. The little
Girls watching had the hems of their skirts
In their mouths.

El Greco would have made it a sketch in charcoal:

The boys in their aprons, a great oak scaffolding,
Rope ladders, stick-ladders, and bald priests
In their black gowns scurrying about
With a dark filigree of gold and silver.

In the foreground there would be a twisted
Plane tree, two firs, and a red waterfall.
The sun is a wheel in the background. There are
A man and a boy rising. But rising

To a parlor with an old blue sofa.

———•••———

I am trying, now, to bring *you*, one last time,
Up out of the ground.
There are bells. This is not old Number Nine
In Websterville, Vermont, where I dropped pennies
And waited, it seemed for hours, for them to fall
Onto the quarry floor or into its green pond.
The hills smelled of gunpowder. They were shaded
With the old rigs and derricks. Small trees
Grew from the sides of these holes. In the shadows
I could spot you wearing your gold suspenders.

You spoke French at the table. For breakfast you ate
Steak and the greens that had been boiling

Since before the first light of morning.
In the stonesheds you lifted the heavy
Iron pencils and chisels. Granite slabs marked
In crayon and chalk.
The yellow papers with inscriptions: *In memory*
Of our small daughter who had hazel eyes and
A flower for a birthmark.

I was in Vermont this summer, and one afternoon out
Walking for milk I crossed through a cemetery.
Young men the night before had come there
With sledgehammers. They knocked over the marble,
Granite, and greasestone crosses and breadbones.
Their sleeves rolled up, their dark hair
Swept back, in tight jerseys they attacked something.
What made them? What made Guido, the Italian
Stonecutter, work point-delicate mint and juniper leaf
Clusters into the high arches of slate headstones
Going to the potter's field? We would bring jars
Of artesian-water up to his shed as late as midnight.

The Victorian roadhouses in Websterville are being
Burned to the ground, cleared for new houses.
We build, and we bring down. To be remembered?
Those young men with hammers: there, with the boxes
Under the grass. Grunts and laughter.
Perhaps, they did this often
If there were no girls along, who were bored
And unbuttoning starched blouses.

I remember the women
At the booths: the clear bells and sirens around
The hills in Websterville bringing all of you up

Out of the quarries for supper. Up out of the ground
You were all frightened of. And

In that German painting of a forest, a woodcutter
And his son with axes over their shoulders
Are walking beside a pond. The son's reflection
In the water is larger than his father's
Who is placed nearer to the pond.
The cascade behind them
Is red with a sunset, so is all of the water.
Grandfather,

The living and the dead are both one. And another...

IV.

I can't sleep! All evening my wife has washed the walls.
That wall reminds me of a woodcut: Chinese with dark braids
Are dipping into a tide pool,
Into the yellow reeds and sea grasses,
Searching for the nests of ocean pigeons, the blue fledglings
Captured in nettle baskets just as the tide
Reverses itself under an opaque moon.

I want to visit Mexico! My quartz-lamp
Is still glowing in the corner, it has a tungsten filament
Behind oval windows with a pink bromide fog.
Flaring up beside a broom of asters.

The pear is half-eaten, the scotch warm.
My poems and my photographs are not warm!
My wife is sleeping. Now,
I see on the walls reddish-fawn caracals;
These big cats fell into bird-nets in India.
And all over Asia, the British in their stone barracks
Played a game of skittles
Where two caracals are loosed

On fat feeding pigeons inside a circle drawn with lime
And these birds, these heavy birds, break upward
While the two cats knock down ten or eleven
Of them in just a second: the pigeons
Gaining on their wings, the spitting cats climbing
Six to seven feet into the air and scoring kills
Up there, all eight paws erasing

The rising flock. Behind this gaming and
The screaming soldiers, a dark boy with a pole knocks
Melons from the magistrate's vines.
The hurt birds and melons on the lawn are left
To the curiosity of yearling goats. What reminded
Me of the caracals? The desert phoebes
Outside my daughter's window?
The water on the wall, or Edgerton's eddies of
A tennis stroke, his *Wire Struck by Bullet*?
The silver and dark abstractions of the stop bath

Giving up, earlier, in the black closet? The scotch when warm
Makes me want to return to the pear, or the icy melons
Downstairs that were a gift from two sisters who posed
For me last Wednesday.

I photographed them in hoopskirts.
They formed a tent.
No, they formed a human jewel. For a god
With teeth

Like the Tibetan *dakini* with her caracal mask and monkey's feet.
She would eat
The temple birds with both hands like sopping melons. In Tibet
Desire was a dark red smoke, sunset, or
My pen-and-ink asters: their radial spokes and all their
Pinpoint sexual organs turning toward a lamp

As pigeons toward a monk who's spilling seeds from his deep robes
That fold, over and over, like tidal water
Turning, at midnight, in a secluded cove...

      v.

for Kaya

Outside the desert window-gate there are
The heavy legumes that flower: the ironwood and mesquite;
In the Joshua tree there sits a broken doll
In a satin dress without sleeves, she
Seems sovereign in a small riot of birds, she
Watches over them and my wife's dying rail of oleander.

She is a morality for me.

Tomorrow, I am fifty-two years old. I still
Believe in work, and in the adoration
Of children. I remember the *hieros gamos*
Of the Byzantines, the Madonna lodged with the child
At the axis of the mother's body. No sentimental
Reclining boy for them! Aztec poets

Were begged by their Princes to write a few dark verses
For the backs of all their mirrors. These poets
Were rewarded with jewels and fruit. If you won't beg me
To tell you why the doll is in the Joshua tree.
If you won't bring me fruit on leaves. If you
Won't bring me a goat with its sweet, white curds.
Well, then, I just won't say what she is doing
In her tree.

So, admit it: *the days seem shorter.*
And, doll or not, we have forgotten something:

If you are going to climb up into trees, you must remember
Where you placed your hands, your feet
And descending

Repeat these positions in reverse, never looking farther
Than that branch which supports that foot most
Advanced in your descent.

Now past fifty, I teach my granddaughter, who's afraid of trees,
This same technique.
And growing older I hope she lives with grace. *With trees.*

VI.

after the murals & bottles of Dina Yellen

The new for us is the last thing our worlds
Have forgotten, brought back by someone, not

Out of necessity, but
Out of *the otherness* of invention which has an unforgiving
Mother, and *no father.*

The dreams you would have as a girl when you would sweat
And then wake, screaming. What you saw:
A white umbrella,
The primitive mural on a cave wall in woods in Sweden,
Votive tablets, the ancient Oseberg bucket,
The Sumer Warka head with its pitch-black, feminine mouth
And silver libation cups. Or the vermilion ladder, lotus
With water at the middle: its six petals, each
A syllable. And, once, in the afternoon,
A bull's genitals beside broken, chalk pencils.

The terra-cotta and indigo flowers that climb as rope
Up your bottles. The bottles, a clay that's dark as basalt.
The serpentine mural that is larches in winter.

The other mural
Is a procession of animals without human companions:

The mouth of the fox holds an onion that is red like apples.
Roping up the bottles is the viscera of a dead oarsman.
At the wings, a little of the blue of the Mediterranean.

A November night at your studio in the marshlands
Of Vermont: the kilns outside glow against the pines, there
Is lime around the ovens running to snow:
You remember as a child looking
Past the mica window of a woodstove to where you saw
A sun, the sun that the Aztec poet described as having one
Flower which is black! Black like Paul Klee's *Moon Flowers*
In its silver-wrought frame which was discovered by G.I.s
In a munitions-underground the Nazis
Built as an art treasure for a new order of things.

The Nazis who may someday be forgotten, who then will be
Brought back again by someone, not out of necessity, but
Out of a longing for *an otherness,* which will have no mother,
And an unforgiving father!

VII.

a painting by Odilon Redon

This strophe takes for its subject a secret
Of Mademoiselle Violette's, who is just sitting
There in a thin dress in a heavy arrangement
Of blue and yellow flowers.
Somewhere between her small powdered breasts
There is concealed a letter, some
Pressed francs, a rose petal, and
A perfectly clear bead of sweat which like a snail
Inches slowly down to her white,
Flat stomach.
It tickles but she doesn't flinch:

This schoolgirl sitting in a bright room
With all the windows closed: a sweltering
Afternoon in August. But the girl's poise
Is a kind of courage, is like
The refusal of the painting to be important, and
Is the subject of my strophe which
Like a sad failure at sex
Accepts failure as a kind of accomplishment.

VIII. GOOD-NIGHT MRS. CALABASH, WHEREVER YOU ARE

I'm going to quit this! These pages like walls.
At night, lately, I've tried to photograph
A watermark. A watermark
Like a good-night kiss. The beer and scotch
Have stained the old bureau cloth.
I'm not unhappy with my diary—I'm not
Unhappy, just conscious.

I've drawn
A line between myself and what the moon,
In phase, will do to the limes like green eggs
Up in the leaves outside; will they ever fall?

Stieglitz's pears up in the branches
Like heavy sandbags in a gymnasium.
The shadow-boxer cornered by pine boards,
There's steam coming from the baths.
And sweethearts—why not a poem, also, for boxers?

It's Sunday morning and Stevens's walrus form is
On the wall—his wonderful pigeons settling
In his poem. The deer walk through clearings
Blinded by the phosphorous lights
Of a little lichen on a rock. Still dark outside,
My pigeons rise and volley in the sky
Above caracals.

What's the figure of morning on the walls?

I'll go to Mexico this winter. I'll miss you.
There will be no coal in the cellar.
The jars will not be filled
With the long body of cucumber. But
There will be the icy, white spittle
Of snakes on the windowpane.
The first frost as patterns thrown
Against a wall. I'll sleep now:

A watermark, the kiss that is a fossil;
The firm muscles in the lips
Forming

Like a fist that passes through a plaster wall.

Hours, and I was wrong! It wasn't a watermark I wanted,
It was the cutout of the Matisse mask, a triptych
With dark eyes in the border panels and in the center
A dusty nude, the snow figure

Of a woman with wet grape clusters for nipples.
She should belong to the Russian legend of the snow orphan.
Along with the flanking eyes I could add, in pastel,

The counterclockwise lion-bird parable: Sumer,
Not the early third millennium B.C.E.—
Should this triptych show a fear of portals! I think
I am raving again. I finished the odalisque, it is
Pink from exposure to the lamp.

As a child I would freeze before the gargoyles
At the door to the Public Library. What I mean is that

The Sumer photograph should be erected by mules and exiles
Here in our desert.

When Coleridge said that his mind was swimming again, he also
Asked if it was by accident
Or in fear of the event?

They feed opium to the milkfish in their dark
Blue estuaries in Asia? (Coleridge should ask
The female milkfish, who is swimming with her
Seven million young in a pond outside Peking, *What's wrong?*)

For a week I haven't dressed. The windows are blocked
With wet newspapers. I am not depressed.
None of this is
My mother's fault. She is called "Susie";

As a young woman she opened from within while
Closing down around a small, red construction
Of mucus, hair, and bone. Someone was growing inside her:
Stealing from her
Calcium, protein, and the former calm
Of her mornings...

Winking at robins, what advantage
The unborn have lounging on that warp of bone
Like the grown man sulking on this dark watery divan
            one late morning, and throughout the afternoon.

"Gently Bent to Ease Us"

for Bill Knott

The rainmakers are these second growths
Of color above the high cane fields of the peninsula.
A cold air in banners crying to the turquoise sky.

And the poets die blowing
Flame through a heap of red twigs. The magician's
Words like waterfalls beyond the salt marsh
Making a bird nervously rise
Out of its poor delight in wild autumn mustard.

The red plane climbs through thunderheads
Dropping now to a bright city and its plateau. The mud
Of the Yucatán slowing the river.

Back in the thick growth oxen are farting
In gladness that the plane kicks its amethyst air
While carrying letters, beans, and dark bricks of tea
Beyond the open abattoirs of sky burial
To the dead who are sweeping
Abstractions from the narrow twilit streets of the city. The

Twins are painting the night leaf.
The jaguar like a union-boss shredding sheets of music
In his maw, gesturing to a striking orchestra…

It's an old opera that leaks…

Mad Pescal, in a diary, said, "It is
All the literature of stone, where puzzlement
Alone buggers the dream merchants
Of a northern kingdom: they enter the ball court

In a ceremony of cold sandwiches
And algebra."

There are no scorpions in the hanging gardens
So the ancestors will keep their places
Across the killing grounds
Where wind lifts ashes
Powdering the sleeves of trees
Like an archer who pulls the bowstring
Until it reaches a mole
With a white hair on his cheek.

The arrow streaks in bright parcels of arc
Above the planet, oxygen
Singing through gaping teeth,
The little sternum buried in our forehead
Strumming like the Inca on a waterlogged packet-boat
Heaving past headwaters while crossing
The *t* in the trapezium of Orion; let them

Fuck each other forever—
Dogstars like pulsing tin in a summer's heat
Decorate a poor aria of widening nebulae
Where the filthy costumes
Of a tenor fall at his feet and the young soprano
Beneath the ropes and colored sandbags
Lifts her naked legs—her toenails painted
An iridescent green, they rest now
On the hairy chest of the tenor
Like the emerald gear of a long-dead martyred king.

Poem for My Friend, Clare. Or,
With White Stupas We Remember Buddha.

So when the gods wearing their colored cloaks of nearness
Passed, their indescribable rags, even shitted in the back, passed...

And they were begging, not for forgiveness,
But for a lavender coverlet, soup with old bread,
Or, of course, the rent...

To tell you the truth, it's my friend's friend,
A woman all alone with her children
In a cold room in Chicago, who has left the gods insensible
Even to the digressions of intestine.

I too am sick to death of my own self-righteousness.

To tell you the truth, when I'm desperate
I take down the green shoebox
With the creased black-and-white photographs
Of a childhood in Maine.

I show them to my dead brother.

I cry, while seated gloriously in my forehead,
The witness nibbles at a pear, lecturing
On the desalination of this planet's seawater. Now,

With a fever and a flashlight, before the mirror,
I peer in at the swollen uvula at the back of my throat.
I say to my friend that
It looks like a horse's penis dragging over the earth.

We are all
Very self-absorbed and eccentric. It's troubling,

But before the Buddha lived, there were no Buddhists!
There could be none after him. When he was dying

His disciples asked how they should remember his teachings.
Weakened with dysentery, silent,
He struggled to place one black begging bowl
Upon the empty face of another. It was unmistakable —
Like an onion. "Forget me, save yourselves." Or,

"Here's a beautiful postcard of five white stupas in Nepal."

Bells in the Endtime of Gyurmey Tsultrim

The bowl made from a tobacco-yellow skull
And the blood of a yearling ox
With seeds of quince floating in it.

An airliner

Flying low over the marshes
Of a thousand purpling ducks,
And the white dirt of ducks
Over the potato fields.

The lightning starts in granite and forsythia scrub,
The missiles of nettle
Rising in dark sky. Animations of a night bureau
And cedar boards around the dead poet's button accordion.
Emphysema of sound

From the stars
Where we follow the fires down to the ground.
The lightning-scrawls
From boulder to pasturage
To a horse-chestnut tree — *cry of killdeer* —
That stands like the government agent
With ears of the Buddha.

Sprays of rhododendron
Across the caskets of French merchants,

Their daughters, and the stewardess
From Marseille who hurriedly
Washed her speckled breasts in talcum.
The breath taken away
While her wrathful guardian,

A funnel-bird that climbs into the wind
Plowing air over the North Atlantic, tips —

Orange fuel running to the fires.
The black box intoxicated with quiet.
It falls into the sea.
Carbuncle-rubies in the mouths
Of the dead who are swimming toward me.

Charlie Chaplin under a canopy
Of oaks, this poor light
Of the street, where he drags
A burnt, open suitcase along a cobbled relief…
The white length of it unrolling:
Butcher paper with a kindergarten's fingerpaint
Imbibing it.

Charlie studies a children's augury:
Fresh pond, red trains, sled dogs
Moving their bowels in harness…
A diagonal sleet.

He is ignoring the small boy
Who runs ahead of the milk truck
Delivering newspapers
To the porches of the neighborhood.

On the front page below the index and weather
The platinum ink of a man standing
In a Mercedes-touring, in Rome:

Some goitered gnome, anti-Christ
Of the suburban twilight, waving to us — saying:
Friends, I am the lightning strike
That starts with sky, lake of fire,

Dry and erudite — awaken, husband and wife,
We are now mice in the field
Frightened by the orange fattening crest
Of three small fires circling
The wreckage of a blue-and-white Cessna:
The great folding lung of the accordions
Sending a message
Out of the phosphorous afterlife
Of our rising sun.
                    Something has begun...

The Clouds of Magellan
(Aphorisms of Mr. Canon Aspirin)

a prose poem for David St. John

I.

I once dreamt that Cézanne lectured on the circumnavigation of a pear.

*If Einstein corrected Newton by disputing the merely local and if an
exotic lamp of projection in gravitational lensing leaves Einstein's
theories somewhat restricted to our solar system, then I predict that we
will progress toward a hyperbolic quantum fact that will have its
verification in the floss wood from which Bottom wakes to make his
most wonderful midsummer speech.*

If you are the village idiot and the village genius, then you will
be sacrificed.

They will tell us again that the metaphor is a reconciliation of two
disparate things. They have misunderstood something.

Samson struggled with hundreds of foxes, pairing them at their
tails. He placed a flaming brand at each knot and sent the foxes
down into the dry unharvested cornfields of the Philistines. The
shocks, standing fields, vineyards, and olives were now burning. The
Philistines saw that metaphor is the joining of two similar things.

You must send fire, without props, from your mind to the mind
of another.

Rumi thought, "If you are a friend of the Creator, then fire is
your water."

Clerks are not in the possession of metaphor.

Two foxes joined at the tail are a parody of fire. Two burning foxes joined at the tail are fire.

Kierkegaard bore a likeness to the Hittite god of taxidermy. He lived in the realm of IT.

They have told us that simile is a weak thing. I don't believe them.

The seven dimensions of the string symmetrist remind me of the religious legend of the seven laughters of God. The first laughter, of course, was light.

God enjoys us just as we enjoy the dance of the Spring calf. (We eat the Spring calf.)

Once before in silence we condemned Kafka to the mythology of the libretto, judging him a common hysteric. We are charmed to think that Auden's treason of clerks is inert. Or worse, that Melville's Manhattan and Kafka's cat filth are beside the point.

There is a binocular weariness to all the visions Eliot and Wystan Auden showed us in prose.

What no one ever told you about that passage in scripture devoted to Samson and the brands is that in addition to the running colors of fire and foxes over the land, in addition to the hot wind that sucked breath from the lambs, there was also, at the height of the cornfields, a transcendent storm of white exploding seed which had religious significance even for the Philistines.

The four terrific agents of movement are earth, air, metaphor, and water.

During the Russian Civil War Sergei Eisenstein watched a horse in snow being eaten by three men. They tossed white bones over their heads like an aristocrat digging into a chest for her red dress. Eisenstein observed that while the men were feeding they acquired a certain happiness that resembled exhaustion. Much of the horse was within them, and had become them. Then Eisenstein in an act of love devoured the three men, refreshing the four horses of legend.

Happiness is not an acquisition. At best, it might be a sad acquisition.

I prefer Coleridge over Shelley. Unlike Coleridge, Shelley lacked a rheum of his own.

Shelley was a legislator who ate of the horse. He was not told to first discard the wings.

Wallace Stevens wrote, "The highest pursuit is the pursuit of happiness on earth." Like Shelley, he ate the whole horse.

Wordsworth ate old milch cattle. He was divine.

Wallace Stevens knew. "There is no wing like meaning."

Meaning is a failure of memory. Aleksandra Luria described an amateur mnemonist who remembered whole novels, word after word and page after page. But the man could not forget what he knew. He lived without pattern or nuance. I think Luria's mnemonist was obsessed with the Protestant God who was even watchful of the sparrows. He suffered insignificance. For him the sparrows were a kind of deep grammar, and a torment.

The Protestant God of my childhood was a god of systematic failsafe system failures.

The line in poetry has its origin in the plowed field. This is simply true. Farmers are the natural enemies of government. The farmers are all but vanquished. The poets, too. Wordsworth was a curiosity for farmers. They took him for a happy boob. And never resented his leisure. He plowed the air into dotage, then the heavy leather tack dropped fast like the chest and shoulders of a man just guillotined by the kind of rabble only a large mind or city can produce.

Especially in poetry, revolution is an appetite for horsemeat.

When a dark crisis of memory goes aloft, it is either propaganda or poetry.

The bones of Pegasus are a tapioca of blood and air.

If Joseph Stalin feared poets, so should you.

The Romantic hero has only been clearly understood through the conventions of parody. We laugh to survive as narrative irony points to one structure while insinuating another. It is always poor Byron. They forgot to have this discussion with us when we came to *Lear.* Think of the deconstructionists who expect any day now to be raptured into poets, philosophers, or kings.

Ezra Pound overwhelmed all of his children. How else do we account for the sanity of minimalism.

Kafka mused that when Americans visit a zoo in Oklahoma they are constantly looking over their shoulders.

The country I was born to is not the country I will die in.

All enactments are boring without the light transport of the senses.

Stephen Crane, with no experience of war, listened to the lies of old soldiers, suffered dentistry at the hands of a horse doctor, and made a mandala of a cold blue photoengraving by Mathew Brady. From *this* he wrote his masterpiece, *The Red Badge of Courage.* Later, after real exposure to battlefields as a war correspondent, he wrote far below his own standard. A prodigy with bad teeth—he prophesied that Ulysses would die in Vietnam.

When the Clouds of Magellan were first seen by Ferdinand's sailors they mistook them for atmosphere, but with a passage of nights under the southern sky they soon realized that the large cloud was a solid astronomical arrangement—a galaxy of ten billion stars, satellite of our own path of ashes...

Every imagination must have its pigeons, and someone to feed them.

The dyslexic Flaubert fed his own pigeons. As provision against starvation they migrated north for the winter.

That one night of *Finnegans Wake* makes *Oedipus Rex* look like a pony parade.

While listening to two feminists' mincing abuse of Sylvia Plath's life and work, I suddenly saw them standing, mud-spattered, in Ophelia's open grave playing an enraged Hamlet to a most insincere Laertes. Strangely, I began to forgive them.

Auden has Prospero tell Ariel that it is confining to have his dukedom back, now that he no longer wants it. In Shakespeare's Epilogue Prospero admits to having lost his magic. The two moments combine to make the only confession worthy of a strong poet.

Then I remembered that Polonius was already slain.

II.

for Henry

In my dream a black corporeal bull straddled two remote zones. The bull no longer could fertilize the land it grazed on. A savage inhalation or old reversal of wind had become desperate after an epoch of starvation and like a vacuum literally began to rip flesh, sinew, and bone away from the close jowls of the bull while receding backward into it, reaching the great flanks of the animal. The bull's hunger had sucked the bull inside out while feeding *it* to itself. With an empty sound, the creature had vanished. It had vanished into its own mystical wound. The mouth that did the devouring was just a threshold where the force of gravity began like an event horizon of a black hole to cannibalize the very singularity that made it a phenomenon. Though I couldn't see the bull any longer, I knew that while it was being eaten it was presenting itself in the other zone; now belching its elementary diet, a star giver of universal proportions.

Edgar Poe wanted the fool in *Lear* to fly a black kite. Poe was the first human to realize that starlight was delayed, voyaging, and old.

These last ten years of working with young writers I have found that the poets of real promise are mostly women. Their great fear is that the paving of poetic diction will leave women selling soap to other women.

The last stanza of an Emily Dickinson poem reads:

> If any Power behind it, be,
> Not subject to Despair—
> It care, in some remoter way,
> For so minute affair
> As Misery—
> Itself, too vast, for interrupting—more—

If you want some of this depth-syntax from a poet who is still living, read Bill Knott's *Outremer.*

My daughter explains to me that if a strange race of minimals existed in a world of just two dimensions, my pencil intruding in their world would emerge oddly as a slab of pine wood with a lead center.

One night under cottonwoods beside an Apache creek my dead grandfather, Earl Morrill, visited me. He just wanted to talk under those trees. It was wonderful being near him.

A poet who mistrusts the imagination, or perhaps has none, usually succumbs to the third temptation of Christ.

I think the voice that speaks these aphorisms is a Borges character suddenly startled out of sleep. He'll sleep again, is my only consolation to the reader.

Every muse is a brute.

You want to extract a false confession from someone! Whom will you hire for the job—Joseph Stalin or Sigmund Freud?

Job suffered from having two prime suspects. Nietzsche was of unsound mind and obedient to the point of rebellion. Samuel Beckett, the most elegant of them all, couldn't phrase the indictment. The only successful prosecution of God was conducted during the war years by Emily Dickinson of Amherst, Massachusetts. She was not seeking a higher office.

Beckett gave my generation a new comic book. The colored ink of it is still on our hands. We've returned to the *Macbetto* opera again.

A great bull like a plum has but one seed.

Neruda was an inland sea. He was not the once and future king.

I think of each individual aphorism in this manuscript as *nuage:* cloud, cinder-galleon, smoke in the gullet of the oven.

In the popular media Heisenberg's uncertainty principle is becoming almost mystical. It's a shame. It was not a determinist but a relativist who insisted that the radius of curvature of space-time was proportional to mass. Heisenberg, cranky with either position or velocity, thought that no particle can be plastered to the crosshairs of a controlled observation better than to within the distance that is inversely proportional to mass. With heavenly objects the former distance is much larger than the latter so there is no problem. But while mass lessens, the radius of curvature shrinks. At discrete mass the radius curvature and distance indeterminacy can equal 10^{-27} centimeter, the Planck length. Now, Heisenberg says, "Go ahead, folks, and measure simultaneously both the position and velocity of an elementary particle!"

Midgets were popular at the sites of mine disasters in the 1920s. This was a failure of negative capability.

What the relativists must do is cultivate a nostalgia for Cold War espionage. But they must find some idealistic elementary particle who'll spy on all other elementary particles. Cynically, these relativists must hope that their mole, to please Heisenberg, will turn into a double agent and without the loss of either network. In this way the double agent could impishly reveal the two worlds to each other and without a moment's thought for what is called Control—

Perhaps this is mysticism after all. And with rebel angels.

Coleridge was a fallen angel. There were only two women he loved —his mathematical daughter and the Geraldine of "Christabel."

The reveries of a dreamy unabashed nose-picking in the novels of Henry James are a security against panic attacks.

In the shallows of the hydrogen Sea of Samsara there are monsters of involuntary memory like Rimbaud or Corbière.

If contemporary critics wish to understand Wallace Stevens's processional, "The Auroras of Autumn," they must travel to the Yucatán and prepare for the earthquake calendar of *4 olin*.

Why do I get the creeps when a popular poet tells me the writing of poetry is redemptive? My wife tells me that "the creeps" are neurological. Something like a chilled moving-forwardness of unbearable pace like cobwebs.

Clouds have sequence, but no context that we can believe...

III.

The minor characters at a wedding are often the most interesting.

Young athletes in Maryland are learning tennis with a net that is not down, but invisible. It's made with a clear plastic thread. It's a Zen instruction; and Frost's old definition of free verse.

Good formal verse has fields of accent within it that are often profoundly irregular and of an order of experience we assign to the large grammar of a salty red wine.

In a time of war, the Sioux holy man Black Elk was asked to create an elaborate horse-dance pageant dramatizing his most central vision. Eisenstein would have loved the bill of lading: four cardinal horses of black, white, buckskin, and sorrel. A large bay horse for Black Elk. Also beautiful virgins, six grandfathers, painted roads, a flowering rod, nine rapid drummers, and the sacred hoop. All of it was gathered together to purge Black Elk of a recent signifying terror.

In the midst of this extravagant pageant a wonderful thing happened—Black Elk saw in the night sky a tepee built of cloud and sewn with lightning—his great vision had returned to him and he realized the Sioux ritual being performed around him on the ground was the exact shadow act of what was growing in the sky above him. And then just beyond them there was the Morning Star rising over their camp at the wide mouth of the Tongue River.

The writing of poetry *is* redemptive.

Immediately after war, people have little tolerance for symbols.

Trilogy and *Four Quartets* are great poems. But if they were boats, they would not have carried a single living soul back from Dunkirk.

Lowell's "The Quaker Graveyard in Nantucket" is the best war poem ever written by an American. What made this possible? I would say the greeny-black humor of arrested adolescence and a rough counterpointing that is in the same tradition as Jimi Hendrix's variation on our national anthem.

Allen Ginsberg and Randall Jarrell were heroic anonymous census-takers in the spirit world of mid-Century. Jarrell counted *the innocent* and eventually went mad. Ginsberg worked the other neighborhood and lived long and well like some ferocious biblical patriarch.

In general, Stevens is a better poet than Lowell because of his full recovery of breath which must often be, in poets, the equivalent of a natural intellect.

Vulnerability is a writer's best defense. Why intellectually do I reject this?

That lovely Auden wore bedroom slippers on the subway.

If Sophocles wasn't a humorist, then how do you account for Antigone's mortuary gesture over the corpse of her brother?

My Puritan ancestors would have found the Evil One concealed not in the number theory of a lottery but in its Ping-Pong balls suddenly elect and sentient before the one eye of the studio camera. The contemporary physicist now seems unable to quarrel with the logic of my obdurate and iconophobic ancestors.

The leper who has lost his nose to slough and prays in his dark cave for a new one is common. The leper who has lost a nose and immediately cuts one off a dog and threads it to his face is the robust muse of the late William Shakespeare.

Auden mused that the unreal was unanswerable or just absurd. But he conceded that *a poem must be more interesting than anything anyone might say about it.*

The centrifugal visions of Ezekiel were a denial of desire.

Intending no sarcasm, I must insist with Ezekiel that the search for extraterrestrial intelligence, or SETI, should begin with the human mind for it is the only important ground upon which ETs have set foot; this is, of course, predictable behavior for an extraterrestrial.

> I joy, that in these straits, I see my West;
> > For, though these currents yield return to none,
> What shall my West hurt me? As West and East
> > In all flat maps (and I am one) are one,
> > So death doth touch the resurrection.

This verse, according to legend, was written less than eight days before John Donne's death. It was certainly written in the last decade of his life. Only spirit can write like this — the mischief and courage in it alone are enough to justify a life of making poems.

The idea of an intuitive faculty limited by the organization of our nervous system must also include the geophysical mysticism of our earth, moon, and sun. The ancient Mesopotamians will have a place in the deep future of our physical sciences. Their religious myths will, I predict, prove to be more rational than our own, or will prove to have been all along our own.

And, finally, again: *les nuages atomique:*

I don't believe in the apocalypse any more than I believe in Santa Claus. But on the night before Christmas this phenomenon or myth of an arctic saint delivers countless billions of dollars in goods to the children and adults of our more affluent Christian nations. The Christ of the burning wheel was Kriss Kringle, the Norse god of the new year.

IV.

There is a legend about Christopher Smart that insists he traveled from country tavern to country tavern avoiding the King's Bench Prison. He traveled in a torn, green-and-black gown as Mother Midnight with her fantastik-cat-organ-show. Smart would leash stray cats and torture them individually by touching turpentine to the rectum. These cat-organ compositions were scored or musical. The fact that Smart loved cats is unavoidable. While drunken patrons laughed and the cats screamed, clawing air and the sawdust of the platform, Smart would cry prodigious tears that he mopped up with his yellow horsehair wig. His poem, *Jubilate Agno,* is a masterpiece.

When Smart was in debtor's prison his cat, J., would bring him pigeons and mice to eat. This supply saved Smart's life several times. When a river rat bit J.'s throat, killing him, Smart became inconsolable and remained so for two full years.

Most madness is an encounter with a static fact.

If your work is fresh and especially individual and you are persecuted for this, then your persecutors are slavishly in your service.

Was it a truck, the cat, or a frequent contributor to *The Hudson Review* that killed Randall Jarrell? I think it was the songs of the birds with Siegfried holding the baton.

When I met John Berryman I sensed that he was physically a generous recluse situated in a mob. He was alone shaking in an unlit kitchen of a fairly large house.

It may not be a surprise to many that Margherita Sarfatti, the mistress of Mussolini, was also an art critic who discovered a classical motif that reconciled art to politics.

Work with young writers — never for them.

Seamus Heaney makes a convincing and sentimental apology for Milosz's "Incantation" in an essay titled "The Impact of Translation." In the same essay he scolds Edwin Muir for his realistic vision of those powers that sent Milosz into exile. This is not a problem of politics but of art. Heaney is a very good poet but needs to remember John Donne's flat map of spiritual rigor and fact.

Jesse Helms has a daimon that is best known to us as *The Spirit of St. Louis*—it is a large, metamorphosed capacity for Wagnerian idealism.

Artists must refuse all patrons who are easily linked to politics or religion. There are exceptional times, but with regard to this dictum, ours is not one of them.

Why did the printer's wife say, "Mr. Blake don't dirt"?

Michael Burkard wrote, "Try nothing, if nothing works."

Fred Astaire loved skirts but not their contents. In our time that is what is meant by style.

Auden thought, like Kierkegaard, that the doors of heaven are open any day for a rich man. The way is blocked most formidably for those who are in possession of talent. And Kierkegaard, Auden remembered correctly, was in possession of genius.

He was too serious a religious personality not to have insisted that evil be made bulk in any saintly character of his creation. There is an appalling symmetry to all of his novels. He gave God a bad name, then God said let him be called Dostoevsky.

V. SERMO INNATUS

The naturalists believe that confusion is the mother of metaphysics. They are right, but so what. The proper father of naturalism is Cain with his meager acre of terra firma.

The abysmal is full in the middle.

I CHING

This trigram asks that the ridgepoles sag, that we may dream on mats made from the white rushes...

When Telemachus traveled to Helen, who was not in Sparta, he was by now hysterical with his father's absence. Helen calmed the boy by passing him a cooled tea boosted with primrose, poppy, and datura. It is curious, but not surprising, to think that perhaps Helen's tea ceremony made a junkie of the son of Odysseus:

The pivot or rudder of the father.

The confused tongue of sea grasses.

If contradiction was not the resting place of quests then we would be truly cursed with a language from which we would never be subtracted. Not even in death.

Black Elk thought Queen Victoria was the sanest of the white Grandmothers. He met her, I believe, while traveling with Buffalo Bill.

He would have admired Grant as a warrior.

He would have thought President Grant was a toad to forces that wished to make an interior out of an ill-defined frontier that Black Elk knew only as Mother, Grandmother, and Children.

Louise Glück's poem "Mock Orange" is not sensational; it is not a denial of spirit either but rather a rebellion to which the spirit must subscribe. It is a criticism of the failure of imagination in our ordinary lives and is on a parallel with James Wright's "Lying in a Hammock on William Duffy's Farm in Pine Island, Minnesota."

I would study love only with Borges, Tsvetayeva, and Isaac Bashevis Singer.

I would study hate with Bacchus but only after his engagement to Ariadne. This is entelechy with hot sauce — the real enchilada.

What actually happened in the Malabar caves was no riddle to the gay and brilliant Forster. A violent insurrection of anima has no fantasy for *the other*, and its safest medium, with regard to an innocent public, is the reflecting pool of water, not the echoing grottoes of Chandrapore.

If night thoughts carry symptoms, then Coleridge had them.

When gods rape mortal women is it criminal? Is it less criminal in myth than in a poem, less criminal in a poem than in a painting? Is there a statute of limitations on acts of the imagination?

Leonard Woolf, with credentials, would tell us the correct answers are yes, yes, yes, and no.

The word *grotesque* has its origin in the word *grotto*.

It is possible that the avant-garde in our country's poetry is mostly bitter and weakened, or fat and collaborating. If the latter is true, it is not shocking to think that whatever is instinctually avant-garde and surviving has made a clumsy retreat into literary criticism.

I've watched giant rays devour whole squid who are exhausted from a prodigious spawning. The cross-wiring of fear and sex in humans is a phenomenon of evolutionary memory. All instinct is profound memory.

If anything in the universe is ever allowed to be absolutely at rest it must be the teachings of Aristotle. Or to quote Galileo on another matter, "… either in a state of rest or of uncorrupted uniform motion in a straight line." Kepler was a genius of acute angles of thought; Newton of superimposed, adjacently grown angles which when brought to composition do form a circle that is closed but voyaging. You see it was Kepler who kept Aristotle from the oblivion of the solid state by depicting the composing chaos of all order as not chaotic. Just the same, with reference to Aristotle I'd still zap the son of a bitch. He's the sort of guy the System will never get.

If I were to send out vigilantes on a long hunt for Aristotle's head, I would certainly interview the maenads for the job, but I'd hire Sir Isaac Newton.

If certain poems are to remain alive after the poet has died they must make an even appeal to the spirit, the mind, and the prevailing bureaucracies of that mind. The priests, Chardin and Auden, agree that the pronoun WE is singular not plural.

If you are a writer and something wonderful enters your mind, first thank some god for it and then revise it. (To ignore this advice is to be drawn into darkness.)

If only Wallace Stevens had told Ezra Pound *that poetry is a kind of money.*

Kabir was a weaver. Böhme was a cobbler. Tilopa, a fisherman. We are living in dark times.

Our stars in the heavens slow behind the sun in the deep rut of the zodiac. It is a figure of $1/72$ per year. But over time this notation defines constellations as merely impressionistic and superannuates

all hearths but the home hearth and what fieldstones that radiate
out from it.

Monsieur Blanc is patient with us like a mother, though we are
terrible creatures: furlongs of blood literally rising to the height of
a horse's bridle; here in the dry cold valley of Megiddo. There is
sunlight reflecting off a river of blood to canyon walls. It is that
amber resin light of the old Logos. Now the second law of
thermodynamics applies equally as well to gravity as to matter—
with matter order must mean *complexity,* but chaos must mean
simple or *free;* with gravity all this is dramatically reversed like some
freightless traumatic memory we must carry cravenly from birth
to death.

VI.

for George Starbuck

What does the libido of La Belle Dame sans Merci want with
Keats? She is the tenth muse and no kitten; she wants only what
she has been given by Keats — some emblem of the organic, like
syphilis or TB...

If he died with the odor of sanctity, then did he ever live?

By the twenty-third century scientists will have isolated the
individuating deep grammars of Shakespeare and will convert them
to unique proteins. Then, *voilà,* the Bard will emerge from the pod.
Without knowing it, this is what we always intended when we
spoke of immortality in the arts.

During the French and Indian Wars the rouged Algonquins would
drink the blood of the men and women they had killed; they opened
fresh graves and drank there, even with the cholera bout! They
would then return to their villages for winter and infect thousands.
No matter how you look at it, vampires are not romantic.

Freud's problem with cocaine has evolved into a modern practice of psychiatry that is empty without the administration of drugs.

Picasso knew a prostitute with supernumerary nipples. She twice gave birth, each time to a stillborn infant. The bastard promised her immortality as a transcendent nude of Cubism.

I worked on the wards for years and have no patience with individuals who despise, as erotic, Whitman's nursing practices in the field hospitals of Washington. The very best nursing I witnessed was done by women with an obsession and grace that were both founded in Eros.

Forster would not be shocked to learn that the saint, Sir Thomas More, tortured Protestants up in the trees of his rural estate.

Sir Isaac Newton was warden to the Mint and hangman for his small island nation. It's only right that he should have described the local for us.

If Freud was right about Jung harboring a death wish against him, and this was the cause of Freud's fainting spells in the presence of Jung, then a little knowledge is a dangerous thing.

Hieronymus Bosch was a prosperous, born-again Christian who lived and died in a small village in North Brabant. His talent was otherworldly but *his pitch* was that of a sick advocate who passes out photographs of a dead fetus to women entering an abortion clinic. Do Romantics want to know this?

We are at the moment of apogee in myth again; here we must love the neighbor though there is a clear danger in it.

We are not deterred by dreams, but by the merchant interpreters.

The recurring or habitual dream is the dream relayed...

The last moment of perigee in myth coincided with the difficult birth of Erasmus.

Nietzsche thought it was the impotence of Christian love that kept the Protestants from burning him. Actually it was the cost of fuel and matches. Please remember the "dunkings" at Salem.

If I believe that you are lost, then I must not think that I am found —all hurt is the birth of what is not.

VII.

Chaucer's famous fabliau and burlesque situated in a suburb of London made his tavern owner, Harry Bailey, the only muse I would get down on my knees for in some shameless prayer of petition.

If Descartes were alive today, he'd be dead.

The night before Jeannine and I were married I had a dream in an upper room of the parsonage: I was the only person attending a poetry reading. Down in the pit of one of those physics lecture halls, between the Bunsen burners, Dante appeared dressed like a barber's pole. He told me that chloroplasts existed in Purgatory. This was good news and logical, for *The Divine Comedy* states that there is sunlight in Purgatory. I said as much, and suddenly Dante was replaced by Nabokov. I knew it was a bad trade. Nabokov treated me like a schoolboy, lecturing about Evangelista Purkinje and binary fission in cells and magnets. He was more qualified than Gogol or the priest Hopkins, he continued, to explain to me the irritability of protoplasm. He added that only Dr. Johnson was more suited to the subject. He began again saying that the laws of necessity, or *ananke*, insist that Homer have ancestors who were barbarians. (They indeed ravaged the old Minoans while supplanting them.) By now I had resolved to be silent, fearing another substitution of lecturer. So the unlikely author of both *Lolita* and *Pale Fire* went on by dismissing Sophism and its predictable moral flaw. He said we were standing in King Laius's aftertime. He added softly, if you were to find the median point of a metaphor you would have discovered "the difference"—what humans call "likeness" or offspring. Come face-to-face with the critical moment of equatorial attraction in the metaphor of God, he mused, and you will find me claiming to be the clock's face with all the sensitive workings of a polygraph but with no value being placed on what is true and what is false. To my amazement, I stopped him by saying suddenly that he was that odd protagonist in Bergman's *Wild Strawberries*. Vladimir vanished, and I woke to the sunrise and my parents' catbird singing to an infinite company of chloroplasts—there in the misty woods of New Hampshire.

VIII.

A dead classicist is like an old river unlocking its ice in March.

There is only a moment's hesitation between the disfigured and the transfigured in the late draft of a poem.

Wallace Stevens said that he traveled at night and knew every country courthouse in the United States. No wonder he had an affection for the word *vagrant*.

Akhmatova thought that perhaps all poetry is a single sustained quotation.

I've tried to find Kafka's aphorisms in English with no success. So now I've decided to write them myself.

They no longer teach Borges or Kafka in American universities and not just because they are both white men. But because "the children can no longer understand them."

The truth is no one ever understood them, save the children.

W.C. Williams should have made it a commandment that young poets visit old women who are doubtful both of mind and limb.

Eckhart's sanity rested in abandoning the dead language of the Roman clerks.

And, then, Alan Dugan was right, "Cooled heels do lament the mask of frivolity."

After calamitous earthquakes in northern Egypt, thousands of devout Muslim laborers stripped the glassy limestone mantles from the great pyramids of the Giza plateau in order to rebuild their ruined city of El Kaherah. This is the anxiety of influence and it disturbs the dead through necessity while leaving the living untroubled and proud. This is to say that it disturbs no one but critics and historians who are as free of motive as a carbuncle ruby cemented into the yawning granite mouth of Allah.

It is not Robert Lowell's strange heartiness but the frailty of his nervous system that gives structure to his poems, and this broken array of connections is what escapes Lowell's few imitators, *is,* in its absence, what makes them so uncomprehending and boring. The Czar Lepke portrait is Lowell's *ars poetica,* and motive.

The Rhineland, in Meister Eckhart's time, was a place of good wine, heresy, and extra-Sentients or sexual angels. Rilke's ancestors were happy stonemasons in these parts and adored Eckhart's sermons.

When Orson Welles made his first wine commercial, I realized Falstaff would have found our country cruel and intolerable.

That look on the face of the pseudo-Dionysius, Saint Denis the Areopagite, in the fresco by Bonnat is an odd Rodin-like fact for the Pantheon. Denis grasps his head in his hands not because he was wrongly pensive but because he was martyred by decapitation. His style of writing was oriental, liturgical, and wildly Christian. The Church insists that he never existed. I believe he was the confessor, or muse, to both Saint John the Evangelist and Samuel Clemens.

Eckhart meant to be a sometimes antagonist to the historical Jesus but never to the Christ who was the full *striking* or bell tone that levels giants. William Burroughs has said the same thing repeatedly in his novels.

Alfred North Whitehead was right about the relativists and space-time. He gave emotion to the pure female beauty of an altered dimensionality while still wooing havoc with the rigors of Time—left alone, without Hume or time, he gave the brave lie to that grand simpliciter, the senses.

"Realism" is an improvisation of community life like the great sewer systems of Paris or Mexico City.

Eckhart once said in a sermon, "Happy are those who have understood this meditation—had there been no one here I would have preached it to the poor box." This is the first lesson every poet must learn.

Stevens wrote, "God is a postulate of the ego." He constructed his sentence in this way so that he might use the uppercase *G* in God without any loss of self-esteem or credentials.

Existentialists, except those in absurd theater, were terrified of laughter, while, in fact, those existentialists of absurd theater especially delighted in disembodied laughter. Yet, they too lived in horror of the joke.

Is the voice of the self, the *Ipse*, alone with its own triumph? Do creatures in the vicinity of Sirius and its companion white dwarf write *cogito, ergo sum* on black slate and meditate upon it?

Augustus Caesar would have said, "Of course *not,* you dumb bastard." But he was God.

Novalis thought that a natural death was just a consensus of spirit taking flight...

The Passion is, first and foremost, a story, and we must all as writers feel some natural sympathy for Saint Judas as he is being mercilessly swallowed by the plot.

Browning believed everything I believe about God, but the smut.

The levitating Lamarckian bullet-train of future culture will run on one track and will sail past the edge of the world plummeting us into an ignorance Magellan thought improbable or scorned. As with the nineteenth-century railroads this one will depend for its administration upon the scandal of notorious robber barons. This new experience of a land's-end will be more than tolerant of us, and will, in its every function, depend upon us for an antagonist. It will tell us that Gandhi commanded his two young nieces to sleep in the nude with him and it will insist that if we are to increase virtue, we must first increase temptation.

It sounds like fun, doesn't it? Ask Rimbaud's sister.

I sat at my mother-in-law's picnic table, eight inches away from a congregation of her squirrels, and explained to them that there were a finite number of elephant peanuts in the world and they had exhausted their very large summer ration.

We have always known in some measure what value to place on most forms of love but we remain barbarous to this knowledge out of the fear of a Renaissance cupid who abducts satyrs.

The Hasidic zaddikim in their glad wilderness of God-knowledge would have said that nineteenth-century English ladies who loved *The Song of Songs* were not wired silly to their parlors but rather were keening in the wind for a young naked Corn King.

The hypochondriacal storms of *The Tempest* are more interesting than the diseased groin of Baudelaire. We mustn't say so...

Hemingway would have made a great Norse queen.

Salvatore Quasimodo felt that in Eliot's *The Waste Land* the living are dead and in Dante's *Inferno* the dead are living. This is a brilliant Italian chauvinism.

It is the lucid chemistry of adrenaline that is recollected in tranquility.

Augustus hired Virgil to write an epic poem immortalizing Caesar. What he got was a very elegant joke about Homer. I confess to loving both this patron and his poet—taken together they make as great a fool as Lear or Whitman.

Emily Dickinson's celebration of a power-neurosis would have afflicted all of her children, but she was barren.

It's not that American poets don't have an audience. They do. They are hidden from their audience by the private individuals who comprise that audience and by themselves. This, friends, is the calm stomach of a vulgar democratic want.

Rabelais is a sometimes jolly peasant hoot like Charles Ives. He is the modern engine. He died in a wicker chair while experiencing violent tremors. His last words were—*This joke has passed: I go in search of a vast perhaps.*

Van Gogh was a divine pyromaniacal fetishist. He had a faith equal to the mustard meadows of Purgatory. He defended the chastity of Degas by insisting that *if Degas fucked women often, he, being intellectually diseased, would have become insipid as a painter.* He later wrote, "... our meditations cannot put chaos into a goblet, as chaos is chaotic for the very reason that it contains no glass of our caliber." King Arthur would have explained to the painter, "But Vincent, it is not our goblet." Arthur would have said the same thing about Degas's women!

I can't know to what extent I regret having to say this, but there is very little wisdom left between van Gogh's fear of women and a single autumn night of Armageddon. This is why the Japanese possess so many of his paintings.

An old teacher of mine, Marvin Bell, in his brave new volume of poems, *The Iris of Creation*, wrote this:

> In the beginning, as at the end, there was nothing,
> though "was" is the psychic's verb....

The planet Earth on its axis sustained a new and eccentric wobble with the birth of Erasmus. Everything rushed into the future. From this moment forward we have been questing after the clouds of an unknowing. The valerian plant is our common heraldic standard. Perhaps, communism had ironically collapsed while thinking it grasped this fallen standard. What is next, I suspect, is the social mysticism of the priest Teilhard de Chardin. This signals the birth of a false pope.

x.

The last evening of the Empire is devoted to gossip, not poetry.

Aristotle devoted enough thought to the problem of happiness to spoil life absolutely for all Greeks. They would stay like this until that time when they were once again goats eating chalk off the hillsides above the sea.

Dante's love for lunatic geometries was an expression of human sorrow over the loss of its original sexuality.

Kafka was a clerk like Hawthorne and Melville; he dealt with claims for unemployment compensation. One rainy afternoon he told his boss that all women were like flowers. He had just approved a claim for a notorious prostitute.

Jacques Derrida would prove a fierce campaigner in the present cola wars of Eastern Europe.

When Lyndon Johnson showed everyone the scar on his stomach he revealed nothing but a shrewd knowledge of Shakespeare's sad captain, Coriolanus, and a proper contempt for vile journalists.

Jean-Paul Sartre had a chromatic genius like the sound of a harmonica flattened by the passage of a hundred railroad cars.

Freud recanted after advancing some cruel and futuristic notions about hysteria, but before our modern media are done with us they will have made a strange prophet of him.

The Greek mathematicians refused to make any practical applications of their work. It was a thousand years before Descartes would stand in his great furs beside the frozen river and lecture to the army about the one pebble of the calculus.

If Christ is the prince of hosts. Time stops.

The sleepwalking cosmogony of the Greek mathematics haunted the millennial nights in search of the insomniac algebra of Descartes. They met, well and truly, in the alkali desert of Los Alamos. They are out there together now. And because the darkness is a rationing, they have begun trading dreams for hallucinations.

I watched Black Elk speak to the flies on a drying buffalo skin. He addressed them as cousins. I have so much to learn.

It is the end of the Christian era of Pisces. In gladness, they have stood the philosopher of the insomniac memoir up in snow and hacked him to death. The chthonic whores in yellow rags walk out into the countryside to plant beets. They were our Chorus. Soldiers are searching for ponds that have not been poisoned. There's a meadowland with blood that rises to the height of the horses' eyes; its canvas is thirty-six stadia. The assumption of thieves, sea-going steamers, and whole lemon groves describes the season.

I walked up to the cottage with just firelight inside and saw Blake naked before a stone hearth trying to wash the night from his arms...

I believe Thoreau thought politics to be like the gizzard of an erect dinosaur, a dry compartmental clashing of stones with a slow imperfect magic for digestion that is critical to the happiness of all omnivores.

Youth is an unpardonable (or so the young must think) flight from pardon.

It is my suspicion about life that the first thought, like the last, is a natural aphorism. Say, for example, "Oh, shit!"

In ur-catastrophic terms all the artists in Prague in 1906 were encumbered dung beetles marching on the corpse of Erasmus. It's where and when it happened! The big picture was now atomistically threatened by an air or two of Wagner's, an air or three by Verdi. We are not thinking of two world wars here, but of a new consciousness that phrases a decadence inversely equal to the beauty of Job's ash-heap and certain poverty.

The measure of the power of zero-genesis in any given universe is the number of dimensions it volunteers for more sensible observation. The string symmetrists can solve mysteriously for eleven dimensions, but in this physical world we recognize just three. Time is a blunt and exclusive torusical sheath to dimensionality. It will conceal the full measure of spatial complexity, and this keeps our science and its superstitions from easy madness or contradicton. Yea to the illusory values of the obvious dharmas.

Francis Bacon was a bad man who stole the heretical aphorism away from a tradition of evil men who were Freemasons. Sorry, Tom.

Philip K. Dick's androids are just now counting sheep in their dreams so that they might be aroused from the actual insomnia of a midsummer reverie.

Shakespeare's Bottom, in a confusion of winter with summer, would make a heartbreaking android felon.

A resolute economy of language is often the first charade of the absolute. The opposite is also true.

A critic wrote, "If Marc Chagall were an X-rated poet, he'd be Norman Dubie." What a joy these words are, carried in on a wind from the wintering Polish shtetl.

When Nietzsche cries out, "*O sancta simplicitas!*", he is right there with the ideals of a Kierkegaard, but Friedrich will become a martyr to syphilis, insanity, and quotation marks. So he is more credible than the Dane who died, at forty-two, of a steady diet of edifying legumes, or starch.

Kafka maintained that all confessions are lies. So he indulged himself healthily with parables, aphorisms, and mime.

Freud, like most salesmen, wanted us to be skeptical about our skepticism.

I am an amateur writer and a professional reader.

Sometimes I am an amateur reader and then I am too satisfied to write.

A friend, after abandoning the salts of lithium, said correctly that Blake wanted to make pulp of the Infernal Grove in order to be free of the female ghosts banished from Ulro.

Andrew Marvell often gave Milton's daughters a rest and read to the great man from the Bible just after dawn in their barely lit cottage. One such morning Marvell arrived late, apologizing to Milton; he had ridden eight miles bareback and was weak in the legs from two nights of amazing debauchery. Marvell was dressed in women's clothing. The blind poet's daughters voluntarily gagged themselves with their starched bonnets. Later, Milton complimented Marvell on his inspired interpretation of scripture.

I look at the many Buddhas: crumpled white tissues that lead to a woman widowed just this morning: *les nuages, les nuages*.

W.C. Williams wrote:

> It is difficult
> > to get the news from poems
> > > yet men die miserably every day
> > > > for lack
> of what is found there.

Williams was right to limit the compass of this "sentence" to men for in so doing he has once again spoken in praise of women.

One late autumn in Maine I helped a friend after supper with her chores. We hauled three dozen lobster shells out to a field and emptied them into a garbage pit. Gulls came in from Morse Mountain, settling on spoiled cabbages. They lifted into the low clouds. My friend's father was lost at sea that week; she watched the white gulls in silence and until the scarlet bone-coats in their mouths were all that was visible…

I remember Indian-pipe and rue grew around the open pit. It was sordid.

Emily Dickinson's poems are unsayable. They can only be heard in the mind. There was never a poet like her.

I will never know where I am, but I will know where I am not... these clichés of the palace guards organize in the mind like the lost tribe of Israel.

Emerson thought we are all gods in ruin, but are we not also the ruins of a god—like at Palenque or Musée Guimet, in Paris?

XI.

There are the nine muses of the Cogul cave-painting, or there is the one muse of memory who serves their dancing. The eleventh muse is *Kore,* the terrible. She is a red paint made from ground cinnabar and tree resin.

The Irish thought for centuries that if a local poet practiced satire their crops would be blighted, cows would sour and dry in their stalls, and newborns would suffer a variety of rashes and worms. These peasants were enlightened creatures, in my opinion.

Nietzsche, Keats, and James Wright all died of an infestation of muse, of the bite of *Kore,* the horse-leech Robert Graves described in *The White Goddess.* The horse-leech attaches itself to the back of the throat after a horse has had its drink in the wilderness. The leech swells with blood while giving full voice to the horse. She was also the chromatic tonsil-hammer of Wagner's *Desired Knight.* She could not be flattered.

If the faceted rock crystal is not formed by the igneous mass that surrounds it but by an internal, axiomatic seeding of glass, then Aristotle is correct and the imagination is light, light shaped by principles of light and not darkness. This is how Aristotle laid his successful siege at Camelot.

My wife tells me that the flatulence of cows is contributing to the erosion of the ozone layer.

What did Wild Bill Hickok mean when he said, "Your first muse is your last, gents"?

Caliban's aftertime in the mind of Shakespeare is like Tycho Brahe's last banquet of minced or relished reindeer. With pots of beer.

The false anti-Christs are marked by their desire to be Caesar; this would include Jesus in the event of a Second Coming.

It has been established that on occasion a fetus will mistake its rich placenta for a twin and pass its human existence in a depression that secretly mourns the lost sibling.

The Holy Ghost resolved itself to a companionable flesh, disguised as afterbirth, there on the floor of that corncrib in the midst of Bethlehem's surprise winter census.

One and one make two. Tycho Brahe and Falstaff make three.

In the backwater of time, that zone surveyed by Erasmus, we are about to experience a reversal of psyche that will change us. We are only now situated in the age where the sins of the sons are visited upon the fathers.

We have traveled with the primitive Symbolists, with Classicists, with Romanticists—what is next is the death of the arts or else the lacquered bad boats of Visionists.

The yanked tooth of Falstaff is no longer alive with time, *or*

the pulse of a decaying tooth, which is briefly called *world* by Falstaff, finds its time coordinate in the space placed between thrills and in the resulting continuum. When the tooth is pulled from the jaw, blood and ale following, it is restored to the poverty of three dimensions but also to the health from which it was absented by sensation and morbid dimensionality.

One of Kafka's plans for his future was to become a paste pot in Jerusalem.

Newman was wrong, while speaking of doctrine, to say that the poet makes Truth the daughter of Time. The poet makes Space the daughter of Truth and Time the brother to both.

Lakshmi was the muse to Georg Cantor who put this question, "How many points are there on a straight line in euclidian space?" Cantor's partial response to this riddle was accomplished through a graceful stacking of infinite sets of varying sizes. It was something like the wrecked calliopes of countless exhausted Brahma lifetimes, or a single fading and blossoming of the knotted lotus-raft that supports the sleep of Vishnu and his adolescent lover Lakshmi over the Cosmic Sea.

Kurt Gödel constructed a mathematical model in which his continuum hypothesis could be amended to Cantor's work and to the less novel Zermelo-Fraenkel axioms. Gödel's marginalia alone would swamp the brave minds of Wittgenstein and Bertrand Russell.

Gödel died in a Princeton hospital refusing all sustenance out of a fear that his physicians and attendants were trying to poison him. Among all of the Platonists, Gödel was, I suspect, the most brilliant!

I'll share a legend of Gödel's exile. He, the grandest logician of these past two centuries, spent several years in sanatoria suffering from nervous fatigue; then he fled the Nazis and Vienna for Princeton, New Jersey. That same year Gödel appeared in a government building in Trenton to be examined for citizenship. The official assigned to Gödel began his questions stating that the Professor and his wife had held German citizenship. Gödel interrupted insisting with some anger that they had held Austrian papers. The perturbed bureaucrat dismissed the difference by saying, "In any event you lived under an evil dictatorship that could never exist in your newly adopted country." Gödel adjusted his collar, attempting silence, and then blurted out, "On the contrary, sir!"

Now there was silence until Gödel added, "I have just studied the language of the Constitution; I know just how it can happen, and possibly when!" Gödel was obliged to bring two witnesses with him for the examination, and one was Albert Einstein who, at this point, tried to hide his hands in his trouser pockets but failed. Citizen Gödel left Trenton feeling uncharacteristically buoyant and content.

Our existence is an advertisement for an afterlife where everyone's dentures will stick with filial commitment.

What is the first fib in the Book of Books?

Imagine that many of the known forces common to quantum states, something like gravitationo-weak-electromagneto-strong, were siblings who are told each has a pie before him and that each may divide his pie into as many unequal parts as he wants, but that no boy will get to eat the pie he has cut. Further, each brother will eat only the difference between the smallest and largest portions of the pie he's selected. The one mind of this calculation would be powered by an attraction as strong as Samson.

The ratio of pie that could solve my riddle is the substance of Adam's rib placed beside the substance of Eve, but only at that moment when they are physically joined in the act of creating the fetus Cain—

or love.

EPILOGUE

for k.

That summer night of your last innocent memory was like this greensickness of middle life.

Enough!

The pious putting on of nakedness is dangerous. The loathing of nakedness is dangerous. The nakedness of births and deaths is sacred.

No riot of paint and solemn quiddity for Emily Dickinson. Dickinson's crushing ontology, her theories of experience, came hot to her from Shakespeare's characters, especially those who went in the Second Act to Death Row. Dickinson didn't find her power in the knot that holds the thread while sewing—she found it in an Elizabethan grotesque that drowns children. She wrote:

> Civilization—spurns—the Leopard!
> Was the Leopard—bold?

The Sioux buried their dead in the sky? This too was realism.

If a limitless complexity of all possibilities exists and if God is the one possible simplicity we can propose for all possibilities, then surely God must exist. And, furthermore, God would exist in complexity while we would exist in God. This is not consoling.

The aphorisms of Franz Kafka are like a ghost ship without a witness.

The mise-en-scène where Nietzsche holds a burning candle up to Zeus who has just spilled a sack of hen's teeth onto the floor of their boat is like Eckhart's vision of twelve angels who are commanded by God to slowly pick caterpillars from a giant shade tree on Job's estate.

The muse is an insult like a hammer blow to that part of the brain called Broca's convolution; the gift of aphasia issues from this trauma. It is like the threshing of stars from their husks. It is like the birth of radio sky over Thebes, the jackals fleeing the burning city for a wilderness of desert hills.

War is its own thesis. It is different with peace.

If you work with young writers then you must be a reformed fox. It is not important what you give your students; all that matters is what they take. Over time, it is possible to observe this happening and to know the difference. It is crucial, also, for in the future they will exist and you won't.

I think that marvelous painter and child Rousseau adopted a mask, or lesser personality than his own, to protect himself from the jealousy of other painters such as Picasso.

Proust's life was an examination, a wrong criticism even, of reality. Proust was a great magician. He was often occupied with the final preparations of reality. But it was all voluntary work and a denial of experience. It was a sacrifice made minimal by the fact that every moment he lost bestowed upon him permission to write that moment into an absolute perspective. This rescued Proust as if from the very clutches of some alien vanity I would describe as a nearly crippling preciousness. He looked back to the present moment as if it were the improbable ruins of a concurrent but untroubled antiquity. Joyce was the better writer of the two. Between them they have written more than half of those pages that smart people confess to having read when actually they haven't. Both of these men are sacred and dead. *They fucked with time,* is their epitaph.

<hr />

Wittgenstein, as early as '43, thought that Abstraction expressed itself most cruelly through the shared accomplishments of science and industry; so much so, in fact, that he felt our "progress" through this misery might be lasting, thus bringing into harmony our entire despoiled planet. He may have even preferred an absolute destruction of Earth by atomic weapons to this one world of the future technology. Then, not to distract us, he complained that these two extreme scenarios were actually one and the same.

The Hopi saw Lucifer's blue armies involved with the portage of the Morning Star.

How did Wittgenstein successfully traverse the thin ice of that pond William Blake discovered in the harsh suburbs of Beulahland?

The photoelectric transit is subject to the bias of perception, which is the one solid aberration upon which *maya* and everything else depends. The photoelectric transit is subject also to magnetism. This is not an accident. It is why, in the beginning, man had poles and women had children.

Seal up those things which the seven thunders uttered, and write them not! — *Revelation 10:4*

Wittgenstein was disgusted with Shakespeare's similes. He felt that if this was the work of genius, then it was perhaps the set of all sets — Shakespeare, he concluded, must be a law unto himself! This is an acute, almost electrical, field disturbance for the philosopher often-barren-with-words.

We are the red fleshy seal of God's compact with the interlocutor or Holy Ghost.

The spiritual life in our country is hollow just as a whole watermelon is hollow.

Gnosis is what you knew and forgot, added to what you will never know.

I was asked if this manuscript wasn't a criticism of life. Yes, but it is also a celebration of thought; can you imagine how large a part of life that is?

Only the fact of God can conceal God, in-and-of-itself.

Exodus is Greek for the going out into wilderness, for the dressing of feet in the vast escarpments of imagination. One step forward, then another, and we are free.

The pig-which-is-not-a-god can be a pig. Joy.

The god-which-is-not-a-pig can be a god. Sorrow,

and peace.

August 1, 1990
the Adirondacks

A Genesis Text for Larry Levis, Who Died Alone

It will always happen—the death of a friend
That is the beginning of the end of everything
In a large generation of sharing
What was still mistakened
For the nearest middle of all things. So, by extension

I am surely dead, along with David, Phil, Sam,
Marvin, and, surely, we all stand
In a succession of etceteras
That is the sentimental, inexhaustible
Exhaustion of most men. It's like

That rainy night of your twenty-eighth birthday.
A strip-joint stuck in the cornfields
Of Coralville, Iowa.
Big teddybear bikers and pig farmers who were
Not glad to see us: my long hair,
Your azure, Hawaiian blouse, and David
              ordering gin—first in blank verse
And then in terza rima with an antique monocle.

The exotic dancer with "helicopter tits," or was
It "tits on stilts," was not coming—a flat on the interstate
From Des Moines; her breasts probably sore,
She sat out the storm in the ditch
Feeding white mice to the boa constrictor
Who shared her billing.

So you jumped up onto the jukebox and began
A flamenco dance—all the sharp serifs showing a mast,
An erectness that was a happy middle finger

To all those unhappy gentlemen
Seated there in the dark with us.

I walked over to you, looked up —
Begged you to get down before they all
Just simply kicked the shit out of us. You smiled, sweetly gone.
The song, I think, was called "Pipeline"
And the platform glass of the jukebox cracked.

I said that if you didn't get down
I'd kill you myself. You smiled again
While I aged. I said
The elegy I would write for you would be riddled with clichés!
You giggled.

So now you *are* dead. Surely, Larry, we've always
Thought that the good should die young. And life is a bitch, man.
But where was that woman and her snake when we needed them?

The Amulet

for Laura

Blackbirds are scribbling in the winter heat of the trees.
You are accompanying reindeer over frozen water, a large cow
Collapses along a rising incline of rotten ice
With hundreds of animals, now both quick and shy,
Pushing you over into the pine woods
And then nearly into a darkening sky.

But the moon is lowering its threads, lucent with fat,
Into this dream you are sinking with,
And here among the night fires you begin to worry

That the one moon passing like a needle through
The dreams of so many will no longer
Carry a sun. The cold dogs are barking.
You said that you woke, that you were both hungry and naked.

Then, you said, did I wake you? I'm sorry
If I did.

"Somebody'll Hav' to Shoot Ya Down"

Charlie Parker running a towline
From a red barge
Straight to a worm in the gut of a living starling.

The worm like segments of water
Colored with a nickel leaf of tobacco.
The barge with a cargo of potatoes. The pilot

Pissing into the river watched his oldest daughter
Die of a fever. The first polio epidemic that winter
And the branch in the water

Is black, Teacher! Perfect teacher,
The sound of the water slapping the night barge
And the cries of the bargeman's wife

Are not the two wings of some speckled bird
That carries the opening of this poem in its stomach.
"That his sax was a fact"

Is what the bargeman wants to say, pissing
Into the river, no longer
Able to remember the circumstance

That led him to marry the younger sister
With the thick orange braid. It was
She who moved through the leaves

In a bright blouse, who spit
Snow into his ear that early winter.
She would spell *rhinoceros*

Aloud in her sleep
And then "a little used word," *thanatos,*
Which is Greek

For the peace
That is beyond the grave like a great granite keep.

For Milarepa, in Ruse, on Rice Paper

These farmers dressed in gold and blue
Are drinking a heated rose water
Next to the padded window,

Sun and snow
Souring down into the river…

The plow on the hillside
Says to the poet, "Fuck you."

The pink girls in the pear tree
Are substituted
For ideas of heaven
(The local English governor drunk on plum wine
Says that the making
Of lines in verse was first
Learnt by turning back
The plow in a small field.): I cry,

"What shit." I think it's all
Measures of breath mocking us
While we chase

The crazed bleeding roebuck
Over the horizon
Into an even stranger village

Beyond parenthesis.

No narrowing road to the North. Maybe
A passage of light
Described here by lives devoted to the mustard gloriole

Of the fallen pears that are not unlike
The black teeth of the river's mouth.

Like emperors
It pulses around an average value.
Learn that it is all uncertain. Yet, these pink girls
In their pear tree will be forgiven.

On the Chinese Abduction of Tibet's Child Panchen Lama

The commandant, Black Chen, has walked
Across the pastures in his yellow thong
To bathe in a summer stream.

Resting among the caliche waters,
In the roots of blasted trees,
He sleeps, a wild application
Of leeches
Claiming his face, chest, and knees…

From behind a large gold cloud
With a thousand red eyes,
The noon sun warms the swollen leeches
Speckled with increased appetite.

Black Chen wheezes in gnarl
Of bottom willow. The yaks, beyond scale
And perspective,
Like risen black rugs
Are moving over the field above him.

A boy lama and his small family
Were abducted among lanterns in the winter night
And are, perhaps, alive — huddled prisoners
Of a new superstition of rice.

The boy's uncle was shot
In the first year of famine. He was wrongfully accused
Of stealing a carburetor from a green tractor.

His wife was seen walking naked into trees.
Can still be seen

Praying in the foulest cremation grounds —
Smoke rising from her shoulders.
She is adorned in the full glamour of human bones.

Who contrives that like wild rice
Slugs have fallen to a stream
From the skirt of berries and scrub?

The cries of the commandant
Are now reaching his young guards
In the narrow ravine
Above the gate and checkpoint.

An old hag dressed in a necklace of bone, shaded
With age and lichen, reaches down
Lifting the commandant, mucous plug
Of hair and blood, out of the water.
Singing and with a heated stone, she howls
The leeches out of their absolute feeding.

Chen, weak and angry, spits on the earth.
He crosses the field, his arms
Waving in sunlight,
Transparent body with blue ribs, sucked
Meat of an alien fruit. He is making vows

In the air with his hands. The men
Running to meet him drop their guns.
In amazement, they are running
To welcome Black Chen
Who is returning to them
From somewhere they believe they've never been.

The Shadows at Boxford

It's not the white powder cauliflower of still-distant moons.
Maybe just the old salacious
sump of salt pork frying with milk?
It was, she thought, the *modus operandi*
for alien abductions
that became a predictable motive
for verse. He says

he's going to the corner for Lucky Strikes,
a quart of lemonade, and collard greens —

then simply vanishes from our planet.
The summer anniversary
of a suddenly dead cat. The old lady
in a faded denim print walking back from the road
in the dance of the somnambulist.
Then shelling the colander's yellow beans

for her poor chowder of potato with skins.

He's reached the corner and is smoking
with a childhood friend.
The cloudburst was sensitive even to the phrasing of their sentences —
under the green and purple awning
he resumes his speech...   the shock
struck her in the neck. And

how she stayed by him without
attraction or a single thought of gain —
buried his children, mowed his lawn
and the church's —

all the while, in the lower registry
of voices,

the one loafer flung past the newspapers
filling with rain.

The Reader of the Sentences:

... who desires a desire
limitless like the winter lake...

all that's created and creaturely is alien.

MEISTER ECKHART

I.

The dead soldiers rise and walk into the trees.

I smell in the dark wool of the new lamb
the hot switchbacked ozone of lightning—
the two albino elephants of Carthage
making slow passage through a mountain storm,
vivid thunderbolts like nails of naphtha
sewn to their hides and the wind...

           The season of new lambs, Lord,
begins with the punishment of the checkered army
who said, "of this
I am a man, that I am..."

The faded packs of Chesterfields, trinkets of morphine
broken over the ground, fresh blankets,
and jargon rising from the blood-orange gum
of hashish and cold spam.

The white porphyry brick
layering the mountain cataract
contrasts with the spanked water
falling through rock, nothing stops
the large gulls who come inland for carrion and the fresh
mountains of garbage.

Plasmas of gin and quartz spill
over the yellow pastures and long glacial cirques.

The thin Nazi with white hair kicks a table
out from under three partisans —   their skirts
gone bald in a strong sunlight.

Eckhart, this man's eyes were once
plumb with the sparkling waters of the Rhine,
now running just the poor charcoal ink of later chapters —

your one candle finally guttering into the small slate-sink
that makes ink.

Telegraph wires snapping under the heavy snow.

The dead soldiers rise and walk toward Poland.

       II.

The things that are from him, are in him.
Sing, Amen, and

Satan, thus, is without forwarding…
all intimacy began like this?

Not my father, outside Paris, near a village
church where you once taught —

he's cold in wet socks. He and the cook
are listening to opera. Past their shoulders

are ten Frenchmen frozen within sacks —
just more bolts of naphtha

entering the dark? Spent shells
along a hillside picnic and then the S.S.

slicing off four of the shopkeeper's
fingers. His red headed wife, especially her long legs,

being dragged into trees.
Even the tables were dying like horses. Even the leaves

are falling to please them. All intimacy
begins like this.

Winter begins like this...

III.

Again, Eckhart, let's interrogate
the boy attendant to the S.S. general—
he reads Rilke, Monsieur Ancel,
and the young Muriel...   she was bicycling
in the Alps four summers ago. From her
he contracted pentameters
and a lingering sore throat.

Light his cigarette, offer
the Dominican brochure relating ice storms
abating, bright Alleluias and the clairphone, a healing,
levitations, nylon stockings, the etceteras.

He watched the fire race like snakes
through the eye sockets of mules
collapsing with hay,
and the ruptured fuel line of the silver Mercedes
burns now at the roadside—   his general

now living "in the fullness of time"
blackened and swollen, he swells to break:
long boots filling with speckled intestine.

The Beguine women alive in the thousands,
in sack, fasting with sores on their legs and necks
and aware of all things, pass individually
like saints into the oblivion of cupboards.

They glanced once at his burning staff car, its swastika
made of blue petals of paint
flaking into the cold stream.
By sunset, they will have settled
to the floor of a small mountain lake. Like winter

all intimacy begins in detail, and
the thread with which my father had sewn
shut the sacks
has mica in it, was ligature

for the wings of angels, that very last
Christmas pageant.
The philanthropy of the shopkeeper's wife.
Who is now dead
along with the tables, potatoes, horses. Amen...

The Meister speaks, "Both aught and naught
thou must reject
without a trace of image,

time, or space...." —   *Lord, ágaining.   Amen.*

        IV.

The Beguine women slept by the river all summer
for your sermons. That winter
the Baltic froze for the first time in centuries
crushing irreducible salts, oarsmen, and one fey translator
from the Holy See.

The sisters sleep in the poor timothy
still dreaming of a harsh season
that killed half their number. The way

crows broke through the drifting snow—
fresh glass negatives
of the night surf below Gibraltar.
The skeining
bobbins of U-boats
washing up along the northern coast.

Sister Michelle dreamt of baskets full of turnips
brought aboard a gray submarine—
two of its boys
gnawing on rhubarb
in wide straw hats and blue trousers.
Feeling the Sister, though some
four hundred years distant—   the younger one
laughs and picks his nose,
breaking the vision altogether.

She goes down to the river
to soak her feet, to gather snails
for poor soup and paste.

Their boat
was chevron to the local wolf pack; the two boys
are later poached in gasoline and seawater
while the entire French town
watches from cliffs gone vulgar
with limestone and marsh marigolds.

Sister M. sings to the leech at her ankle,
swaying in her ramshackle bliss, "Ashes
to violets, spunkwort to lee…"

v.

Through the lens of water
the already fat leech doubles with her voice
sinking in low maritime tenors —
her dead younger brother, Jean,
from some future life,
waving on a beach in Los Angeles, circa 2012...

The fires climbing behind him, she thinks,
are like the rosy aspirant displays of gill, fan, and lung
belonging to an extant gang of purple raptors
who shit marigolds in a vain parade
of feeding through swamps...

Time folds, she believes. Holding loosely
to the white sleeve of the Virgin.

One of the beasts
still snoring though on its feet.

Eckhart is returning to metaphors of light,
to the white elephants polishing the snow,
long poles with clotted blood on them
like paint pots abandoned on the road
to the outskirts of Rome, to
human torches, further etceteras of divinity,
and the certain depravity
of government obsessed with government...

Eckhart is becoming our snowstorm.

He begins to speak of the boundaries
of pain and sleep.

Sister Michelle taking a tart stick
to the leech on her leg (X ray

of her brother on the beach in L.A.), a
great transport of snow crossing through the chapel
and the distant bell,
familiar evangelist
to marigolds and strong tenors
with holes in their skulls.

I adore
how they are all ignoring us,
with an absolute genius
like snoring.

Eckhart sleeps.

The cold plate
on the table screaming at him to wake
and write something, not

necessarily important.
For his ideas alone

a rival gang of friars
killed him in the winter swamp.
And, yes,
they have dragged
a French woman with long legs
in there with him.
Our martyrs now eloping
with further transports of snow.

The true borders of sleep, Mother,
are the borders of knowledge. She meant, "Please, will you

just let go."

VI.

There are flaws in the candle
like suet or snow
and finches feeding on the ledges
of a stone window, they are twisted
with white seed also.

At smokefall, the ghost of Eckhart
crosses the frozen river and field,
the hooded women following him.

The men who killed them all
once accused St. Francis
of a ruse stigmata flushed with iodine and coal.

The orange gum
of a good ham on their lips —
think of Montgomery in a flabbergast
of peanut oil and spam —   Eckhart cajoling us:
Think of them as the children
of Gypsies

spanning time.

They bring bright spotted puppies to their mother
for suckle,
they eat green grubs out of the rotting board.

In Rome, a quiet one, sits in the dark
burning Corfu sage with frankincense.
Is he their master,
with a lap of coal ash, sage, and frankincense? As a fetus

he invented himself
while live trout slept and fed
in his mother's stomach.

In the flickering light of the large iron lamp
he laughs at Charlie Chaplin
who is attaching a fish hook to string.

This is where his dream becomes strange
for like Eckhart he too thinks: *Tramp*,
and then
adamantine bee-sting,

ozone of struck horn and lamb, rat hairs
and postage chaff in his cereal,
a corsage of orchids and its one nail
of frozen vodka, the mountain witch
descending a mule,
lhamo   lhamo,   while in Russian wheat bins

the junta virus spreads from San Francisco
to the minor Mongolian plateaus:

the flaw in the candle isn't suet or snow.
I regret
that the ghosts of the truly spiritual
are the color of the propane jet,
at smokefall,

while over the frozen river
the galling ball of the sun
nestles in the splayed pelvis of Rhine,
Ganges, the Ohio, and Volga.

His Vatican secretary
with a purple sling over the shoulder
gathering sage on the hillsides of Corfu;

more flabbergast of burning tanks.

As a world, we accuse St. Francis
of a ruse of stigmata
flushed with blood and semen, flushed
with the feathers of the sparrow hawk...

Great marble zones of basilica
collapsing into the lap of earthshake. Eckhart
pleads with the snow wren
                                        to find Francis, saying,
we must think of them as our children?

VII.

The tramps are now living along the pious meadow,
have cut through brambles
and willow root, making
a house out of drifting snow.

Stew cooks in the fire:
the small round bones of rabbits
are balancing in its thick vapors
and, then, midway: the flue-tin
spins like the magus' ruby
that the green knight refused
from the very hands of a nervous Virgin.

At night, they are the brown leaves
scurrying to the door of the snow house;
they are the ghosts
of tramps now huddled
and blowing on their fingers for life...

Sure, Eckhart,
all that is creaturely is alien. But these phantoms

are listening for the summits of snoring,
for the living tramp within...

I've made you unhappy speaking of the treasures
of the poor and their winter storm.
So let's begin again. But this time, Meister,
let's begin, as we said, with the children...

VIII.

for Natalie

The madrigal hay is burning in the field.
Even the horizon is smudged
with his intentions.
Sacchid Plover, the local scarecrow,
is eating a rhubarb pie
while the last of the sun
fusses over angles of snow and stone. The blackbirds

are singing to students of religion in their dark robes
who have settled among the darker trees. Sacchid Plover
looks up and a bomber group
flies over —   sudden black puffs of diesel
and even the sun now
renounces all the Sanskrit words for *terror*.

A great blue heron from my childhood
has greatly lowered his ashen eyelids
and stands in a cold stream on one leg.
He might pray all day like this.

He does not meditate on an only god,
but on the water.
Sacchid Plover has leaned over into our childhood
and yells to the blue heron with prophetic
or wish-fulfilling gestures:

We'll eat the blackbirds. You eat the fish.

All intimacy begins like this.
Eckhart, you were carried into the marshy wood

that was the contented sleep of the wicked.

In the fire sermon you had pointed to their sky.
Like you, we will not die
while drinking milk in our beds. Maybe,
it will be the errand of milk—
But we will have fallen on the stairs and cracked our heads.
We are the happy children of the happy dead.

IX.

The desert stone or Skar-cung inscription
refuses dream
as a vehicle that carries
the religious to their gowns. It says
the shadow of fire has sometimes eaten them
if they were proud.

X.

Eckhart, in a beige shirt, sleeps
just above the snow. Fresh lime
feeding on the icy rose
and the long bones of marigolds.

The reader of the sentences
is lost in the Christmas catatonia
of a Parisian tin and pine erection, or

of the other children in the larger burning city.
The ruby and green Belgique dirigible
hovers over the suburbs while they sleep.

It is early spring of '45.

From here forward there are only ideas
of war. It is the most dangerous of times.

But I have taken the sack of salt
out to the drifting rows of snow. I am sowing
the winter calamus:

the measure is thumb to elbow, tongue
to thumb. No more singing, Sacchid Plover,
there is the day's work to be done.

Last Poem, Snow Tree

after Rafael Alberti

Call a ruined shoe, the sandal—
White, the cow's blood
Forever drained from it.

Where are the happy integers of inventory?

Call the one sandal, abstract and nostalgic:
Glove of the first baseman, it folds like night

Or night's daring bird feeding on amber insects.

The circulations of blood in the snow tree
Remind me of the woman we lost.
The sea rises behind us, at our backs.
Mr. Enos Slaughter didn't die

In Nebraska, of drink. In the snow tree a sick,
Whiter angel picks its teeth.
Errors of snow in water, our names...
You were wrong, Rafael. The stars,
Violent at their tea,

Were the last children to learn the arithmetic
Of memory.

About the Author

Norman Dubie was born in Barre, Vermont, in April 1945. His poems have appeared in many magazines, including *The American Poetry Review, Antaeus, The Kenyon Review, The New Yorker, The Paris Review, Poetry,* and *The Southern Review.* He has won the Bess Hokin Award of the Modern Poetry Association and fellowships from The Ingram Merrill Foundation, The John Simon Guggenheim Memorial Foundation, and the National Endowment for the Arts. Mr. Dubie is currently at work on a long poem in the tradition of science fiction, *The Spirit Tablets at Goa Lake.* He lives in Tempe, Arizona, and is a teacher at Arizona State University.

Index of Titles

Index of First Lines

LANNAN LITERARY SELECTIONS 2001

Hayden Carruth, *Doctor Jazz*

Norman Dubie, *The Mercy Seat:*
Collected & New Poems, 1967–2001

Theodore Roethke, *On Poetry & Craft*

Ann Stanford, *Holding Our Own:*
The Selected Poems of Ann Stanford

Mónica de la Torre & Michael Wiegers, editors,
Reversible Monuments: Contemporary Mexican Poetry

For more on the Lannan Literary Selections,
visit our web site:

www.coppercanyonpress.org

The pressmark for Copper Canyon Press
suggests entrance, connection, and interaction
while holding at its center
an attentive, dynamic space for poetry.

Founded in 1972, Copper Canyon Press remains dedicated to publishing
poetry exclusively, from Nobel laureates to new and emerging authors.
The press thrives with the generous patronage of readers, writers,
booksellers, librarians, teachers, students, and funders — everyone who
shares the conviction that poetry invigorates the language
and sharpens our appreciation of the world.

PUBLISHER'S CIRCLE

Allen Foundation for the Arts

Elliott Bay Book Company

Mimi Gardner Gates

Jaech Family Fund

Lannan Foundation

Rhoady and Jeanne Marie Lee

Lila Wallace–Reader's Digest Fund

National Endowment for the Arts

Port Townsend Paper Company

U.S.–Mexico Fund for Culture

Emily Warn and Daj Oberg

Washington State Arts Commission

The Witter Bynner Foundation

Charles and Barbara Wright

For information and catalogs:

COPPER CANYON PRESS
Post Office Box 271
Port Townsend, Washington 98368
360/385-4925
poetry@coppercanyonpress.org
www.coppercanyonpress.org

This book is set in Adobe Caslon, designed by Carol Twombly, with titles set in ITC Founders' Caslon™ Thirty, designed by Justin Howes. Both faces are based on type cut by William Caslon in the early 1700s. Caslon's designs were the last of the Old Style types that dominated printing for nearly three hundred years. Howes digitized various sizes of Caslon's type from printed specimens and chose to retain the uneven edges for the organic texture of letterpress printing. Book design and composition by Valerie Brewster, Scribe Typography.

Printed in the USA
CPSIA information can be obtained
at www.ICGtesting.com
JSHW082149140824
68134JS00014B/135

9 781556 592126